CW01635751

# SOCIETY 4.0

RESOLVING EIGHT KEY ISSUES TO
***BUILD A CITIZENS SOCIETY***

**Bob de Wit**

Professor of Strategic Leadership,
Nyenrode Business University, The Netherlands

Founding director, Strategy Works and Strategy Academy, Rotterdam, The Netherlands


Inspirational speaker on Society 4.0 and the Digital Revolution

Author of *Strategy: An International Perspective*, 7th global edition, Cengage, 2020

# FOREWORD

In 2017, I delivered an inaugural lecture at Nyenrode Business University entitled *'On the Eve of a Societal Revolution'*. It was based on years of research, lectures and keynote presentations on the future consequences of a large number of technologies, such as artificial intelligence and biotechnology. The main message was that I expected a societal revolution within a number of years. In 2018, I started to write the manuscript for this book, *Society 4.0*, to share my expectations on what our future society might look like.

Halfway through writing the manuscript, in spring 2020, my home country, the Netherlands, went into an 'intelligent lockdown' because of coronavirus. Upon hearing the explanation for the lockdown given by the Dutch prime minister Mark Rutte on national television, I immediately realised that this day, March 23, 2020, marked the beginning of the future I had been anticipating.

With my understanding of the fundamental societal changes ahead, I redirected my research time to better comprehend the coronavirus 'pandemic'. I started investigating the fatality rate of the virus, together with my Nyenrode colleague Professor Bo van der Rhee, by analysing the number of weekly deaths in the Netherlands compared with the years 2015-2019. Bo and I published the results on LinkedIn. One important conclusion of our research was that coronavirus was more infectious than influenza but no more lethal. Why, then, was the world economy being forced into a lockdown? Why would we need a vaccine for this corona flu before going back to normal?

My posts and articles on LinkedIn made me something of a public figure for the Dutch 'Corona Realists'. Then my LinkedIn profile was removed temporarily. I also received invitations to share my thoughts on the virus and possible future consequences. One interview, with Café Weltschmertz, received many YouTube views and appreciative comments. In the interview, which was dubbed *'New World Order'*, I revealed some of the thoughts contained in this book and the feedback I received helped to sharpen my views.

The corona 'pandemic' also speeded up the societal changes I was expecting and so I decided to accelerate finishing the manuscript. As soon as the Dutch government allowed me to fly again, I took off to my favourite writing location: the Caribbean island (and 'extraordinary Dutch city') of Bonaire, where I finished the manuscript. Approximately half of this book was written in the two years BC (Before Corona) and the remainder in the six months AD (After Disruption).

The main challenge in writing this book was to make an extremely complex and multi-disciplinary topic accessible for large audiences, while also keeping the number of pages as low as possible. Armed with the famous quote by Blaise Pascal[1], 'Je n'ai fait celle-ci plus longue que parce que je n'ai pas eu le loisir de la faire plus courte' (*'I write you a long letter because I do not have the time to write a short one'*), I took the time needed to compress a vast amount of information from many different publications into an easily digestible book. It will be up to the reader to decide whether I have succeeded in my endeavours.

***Notes***

1 Blaise Pascal was a French mathematician, logician, physicist and theologian (19 June 1623 – 19 August 1662)

The compilers and the publisher are fully aware of their duty to make sure this book is as accurate as possible. However, they cannot accept any liability for any errors that may occur in this publication, or the consequences thereof.

B + B Vakmedianet BV
Postbus 448
2400 AK Alphen aan den Rijn (NL)

Publisher: Sandra Britsemmer
ISBN 978-94-6215-741-5
NUR 807
Layout and design: colorscan bv, www.colorscan.nl

© 2021 Vakmedianet All rights reserved. No part of this publication may be reproduced, stored in an automated database, or made public in any form or by any means, whether electronic, mechanical, photocopying or otherwise, without prior written consent from the publisher.

To the extent that making copies of this publication is permitted pursuant to Articles 16h to 16m of the Dutch Copyright Act (Auteurswet) 1912 juncto. Decree of 27 November 2002, Official Gazette 575, the statutory compensation must be paid to Stichting Reprorecht, Postbus 3060, 2130 KB Hoofddorp (NL).

Send correspondence regarding citations or reproduction to:
B + B Vakmedianet BV, PO Box 448, 2400 AK Alphen aan den Rijn (NL).

# TABLE OF CONTENTS

# INTRO-
# DUCTION

This book aims to provide both hope and a set of guidelines for a better future society. The society I envision for the future, dubbed the 'Glocal Citizens Society', will be described in chapter 7. The name combines two characteristics of a hopeful future: a Citizens Society and Glocal Citizens.

*A Citizens Society*: Over the past few decades, many global companies (particularly digital, financial and pharmaceutical companies) have grown larger and richer than most nations, while some non-governmental organisations (NGOs) have become more powerful than national public organisations. On a worldwide scale, global organisations and NGOs have strengthened their collaborations with wealthy individuals and 'charitable organisations' to form a new world order of the elite. Yet none of these 'global elite stakeholders' is democratic and their aim is to establish an undemocratic '*Elite Reset Society*', which is described in chapter 6. This is the society that my book aims to prevent, with the ultimate aim being to develop an alternative society with citizens at the centre.

*Glocal Citizens*: Strategic issues and communities are becoming *global*, while citizens continue to work and live *locally*. When citizens combine their local social domain with contributing to resolving global issues they become *glocal* citizens.

In this book it will be argued that whether the *Elite Reset Society* (chapter 6) or the *Glocal Citizens Society* (chapter 7) comes into being depends on how eight key societal issues will be resolved. The eight societal issues that need rethinking are (chapter 5): the nation-state concept, the governance of societies, world governance, industrial capitalism, income distribution, labour, human life and natural living.

This book is meant to inspire everyone to build a better future for our children and grandchildren: CEOs, politicians, public servants, doctors, teachers, engineers, marketeers, designers – indeed all citizens who wish to commit themselves to creating a better future for more than only him- or herself. This book aims to go beyond telling an 'inconvenient truth' and to provide guidelines for organising and realising the *Glocal Citizens Society*.

The aim of chapter 2, *A (Very) Brief History of Societies*, is to provide a historical context for the current societal revolution. I apologise to historians in advance for my very brief summary, but I like to use history to understand the future – not the past or the present – in a concise form. The previous societal revolutions – from the feudal society to the trade society and then to the industrial society – are briefly described in order to understand the revolutionary change from an industrial society to a digital society that will dominate the years ahead.

In chapter 3, *Society 4.0 – the Digital Wave*, the impact of digital technologies is described using a taxonomy of digital technologies. The taxonomy consists of two societal waves: the digital technologies wave (4.1) and the artificial intelligence wave (4.2). When combined, these technologies can have a fundamental impact on society.

Chapter 4, *The Fourth Societal Revolution or 'just' a Fourth Industrial Revolution?*, contradicts the statement of the World Economic Forum that digital technologies are just a fourth *industrial* wave and not a *societal* revolution. A number of fundamental developments are discussed to substantiate the main assertion in this book that digital technologies are changing society.

The current period of uncertainty and change is addressed in chapter 5, *Eight Key Issues for the Societal Revolution*. The societal revolution that comes with fundamental change is discussed in relation to eight key issues. The future outcomes on these issues will form the basis of the future society.

Chapter 6, *The Elite Reset Society*, describes one possible future society. This scenario is based on the extrapolation of current developments regarding the eight issues outlined in chapter 5. In this scenario, society will return to a feudal elite state.

Chapter 7, *The Glocal Citizens Society*, sketches a more optimistic scenario. The aim of this chapter is to describe an alternative and optimistic future society, one based on societal debates that will mobilise societal groups to develop a better future.

Finally, chapter 8, *Invitation to all readers for suggestions*, aims to inspire readers to join and build a 'Citizens Society'. Readers can join the venture by visiting the webpage www.society4th.org. The idea behind the webpage is to form a community of citizens who wish to contribute to the creation of a citizens society for the future.

## The Digital Revolution

Our human society is in transition. We have left the industrial society that has brought democracy, welfare and peace to most citizens over the past seventy-five years behind us. What started as 'just another industry: computing' in the 1970s gradually changed the economy and then our whole society. Over the past few decades, digital companies like Apple, Microsoft, Google, Facebook, Alibaba and Amazon have been growing at an astonishing speed, with Apple becoming the first company to be valued at $1 trillion in 2018 and $2 trillion in 2020. Up until the turn of the last century, the top 10 list of largest companies in the United States was dominated by industrial giants such as IBM, General Motors, General Electric and Kodak. In this century they have been swiftly overtaken by digital firms. In 2017, the top 10 was dominated by digital companies and financial institutions, with one pharmaceutical company also on the list (Figure 1.1). These are the companies that will dominate our society in the years ahead. The big question facing us now is: what will our society look like in 2030 and beyond?

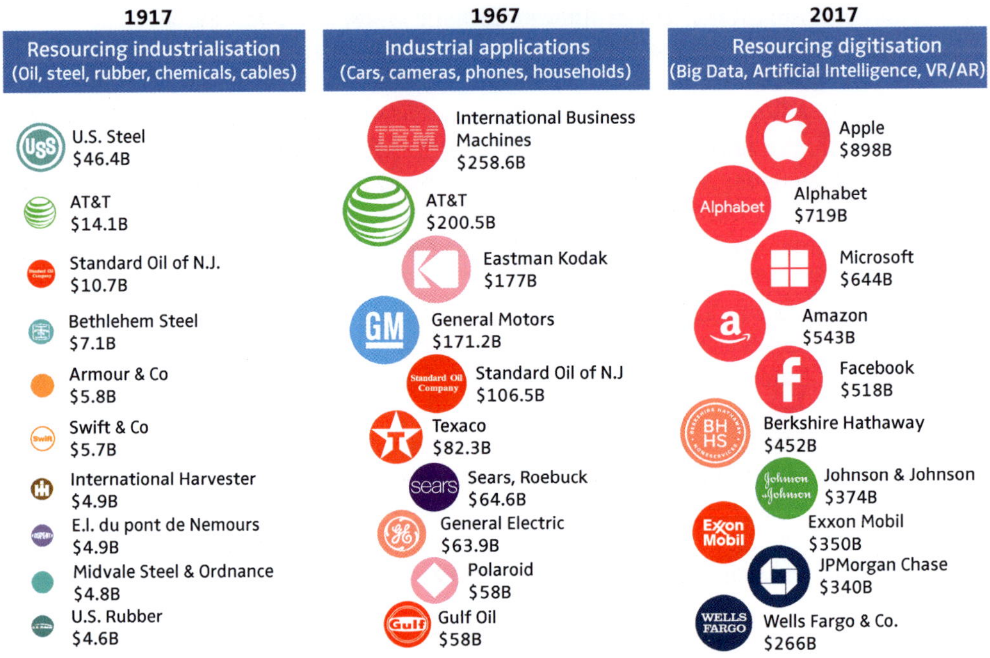


*Figure 1.1: Top 10 US companies in 1917, 1967 and 2017*

A second factor that has gradually been changing our society is that large companies have been globalising to become multinationals. The wealth of multinational companies and their shareholders has exploded beyond the wealth of many nations and, consequently, their influence in the global public and political arena has become significant. Many of them use their increasingly powerful position to maximise their (predominantly) financial interests and behave like 'corporate-states': states that do not consists of citizens but of community members. Under the motto 'Our Company First' almost anything is allowed, including tax evasion, censorship, manipulating national politics and influencing non-governmental organisations (NGOs). These corporate-states align themselves strategically with extremely wealthy private shareholders who act as 'global citizens' with a comparable motto ('My Wallet First') or as 'charities' ('My Values First'). Yet these actors on the global stage – corporate-states, NGOs, global citizens and global charities – are not democracies. Nation-states and public values are mainly represented by the intergovernmental organisation the United Nations (UN), which currently has 193 member states – almost all of the world's sovereign states and the European Union with its 27 member states (in 2020).

Not only will societies change, but humanity will too. The future development of *Homo Sapiens* is departing from the Darwinian evolutionary path. Some humans believe they can and should assume control over nature. Advances in biotechnology, such as CRISPR-Cas9, are enabling genetic upgrades by cutting and pasting human DNA (Sapiens 2.X), while technologies like Artificial Intelligence may soon be connected with human brains to produce cyborgs (Sapiens 3.X). Combining Artificial Intelligence with robots may even lead to artificial beings (Sapiens 4.X).

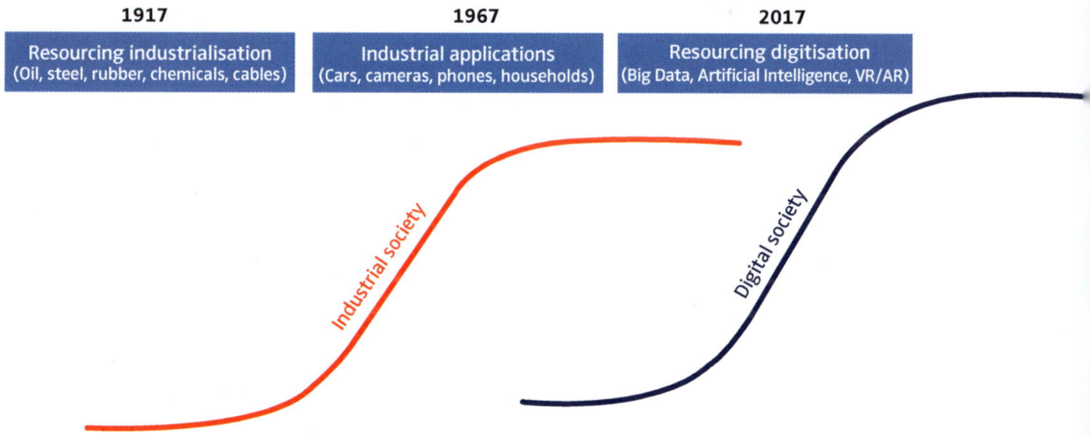


*Figure 1.2: The Digital Wave – Society 4.0*

History seems to be repeating itself in the current transition period from an industrial society to the next society. In the past, increased income inequality and economic crises have been fertile ground for social unrest and sometimes even for revolutions, such as the famous 'Storming of the Bastille' in France in July 1789 and two World Wars in the twentieth century. I consider the 'corona crisis' to be the catalyst for a social revolution that will uncover fundamental societal malfunctions.

# A (VERY) BRIEF HISTORY OF SOCIETIES

# 2

It would not be the first time in history that society has gone through a transformation, as this has happened before – many times even. When hunters and gatherers started to settle the land thousands of years ago, they organised themselves into agrarian societies (Society 1.0); in the 15th century we saw the emergence of trade societies (Society 2.0); and in the 18th century, industrial societies emerged (Society 3.0). With society now changing again, it is possible that the new societal structure of Society 4.0 will be more like Society 1.0 or 2.0 and not 3.0. Or even that Society 4.0 will be unlike any previous societal structure. We could well be the last generation of humans to have lived in an industrial society. So, in what kind of society will our children and grandchildren live in the future?

## Society 1.0: The Agrarian Society

Agrarian societies emerged when hunters and gatherers started cultivating farmland and producing crops at one fertile location. The transition to agriculture, also called the Neolithic Revolution, happened at many different geographical locations around the world: at least 8,000 years ago in East Asia (rice) and, later on, in Central and South America (maize and squash), India (rice) and Southeast Asia (taro). Most relevant as the predecessor of the next societal wave was the fertile region of the Middle East, where agrarian society started over 15,000 years ago[1]. Even today, agrarian societies still exist.

An agrarian society is a society whose economy is based mainly on producing and maintaining crops and farmland, and where cultivating the land is the primary source of wealth for the landowners. Over time, farmers became able to produce more than they needed, feed large numbers of people who were not involved in agricultural activities and stock production surpluses for winter use and/or to sell for a profit. Compared to the hunters and gatherers era, agrarian societies developed higher densities of population in one area with more complex social structures. With land as the major source of wealth, social hierarchy developed on the basis of landownership. Society split into two social classes: a powerful, literate, rich elite that owned and governed the land and an illiterate majority of farmers and poor people without any real influence.

The elite of landowners built a society in line with the interests of their family properties. They formed the ruling governing class and built military institutions – armies – to defend their interests and expand their holdings. Some landowners were warriors rather than rulers, constantly striving to expand their empires. The largest empire in history was the Mongol Empire built by Genghis Khan (1162 – 1227), which reached its peak under the leadership of Genghis's successor and third son Ögedei Khan (1189 – 1241) with a territory that stretched from China to Eastern Europe and from Siberia to Persia (currently Iran).

The social and economic structure of the agrarian society has also been called a 'feudal system'. Adam Smith used the term to describe a social and economic system in which the wealth derived from agriculture is not divided on the basis of created value and market forces, but on the basis of landownership and inherited social ranks. Karl Marx described a 'feudal society' as one in which a ruling class – the aristocracy – controls the arable land and exploits the working class. In the feudal society, there were two separate social and economic groups: a politically and economically strong elite minority and a powerless and poor majority of people. There was no independent legal system; the landowners and the churches determined how people should behave and punished violators quite ruthlessly.

Yet, during the agrarian age there were exceptions that marked the beginning of a new societal structure: trading cities. As societies developed, mainly in Europe and Asia, commercial trade became more important. The excess produce of farmers was traded at local markets, as well as other agriproducts and clothes (such as Chinese silk) from other geographical regions. Trade routes were developed and a number of cities on these routes became commercial communities. These trading cities flourished not because of land ownership and family elites, but because traders created value by developing markets of demand and supply. The city of Petra, for example, located in what is now Jordan and one of the most beautiful places on Earth, was a key junction for several trade routes, including the Silk Road. The rulers of Petra became extremely rich by levying taxes on merchandising activities. Some of these trading cities became strong and powerful 'city-states', such as Venice, Florence, Milan and Genoa in northern Italy. More than half of the economic income of these city-states came from commercial activities and so they were not agrarian societies but commercial societies – also called Trade Societies.

## Society 2.0: The Trade Society[2]

While commercial city-states were not based primarily on agrarian activities, the societal structures were still feudal, with a ruling elite of aristocrats enjoying distinct privileges: political and economic power were in the hands of the ruling class, as was the legal system. In the north-western part of Europe, however, very few cities became city-states. Instead, the countries' societal structures changed. Most notable was the case of The Republic of the Seven United Netherlands, also called the Dutch Republic and currently known as The Netherlands, which became the world's richest and most powerful country

(1580-1621) and an example for many other countries, including the United States. Although there were many trading cities, such as Amsterdam, Enkhuizen, Hoorn, Medemblik and Rotterdam, none of them considered becoming a city-state. And for a very compelling reason: they needed to cooperate and jointly fight several enemies. Not only Spain, from which they had just freed themselves, but many others as well: the Germans in the east, the British in the west and the French in the south were all potential attackers. Yet the main enemy of the Republic was water – especially the sea. Much of the country lay (and still lies) below sea level, as a lot of land had been reclaimed from lakes and the sea. For example, there used to be more water than land in the province of North Holland, in which Amsterdam is located. More than half of the province was made up of reclaimed land. The Dutch had to build dykes, canals and windmills to protect themselves and enable trade routes over water, which provided another good reason for trading cities to cooperate.

The divide between cities and the countryside, common in feudal societies, slowly disappeared in the Dutch Republic. Urban trade activities and rural food production became increasingly aligned. Farmers started growing produce that merchants could trade in. They kept livestock to produce butter and cheese, and also produced hops (for brewing), hemp (for rope-making), linseed (for oil) and madder (for dyestuffs). With this market-driven approach, Dutch merchants gained a strong foothold in European trade.

The big breakthrough for sea-going trade was a large contract signed in 1438 to trade Russian grain using a fleet of ships sailing to the western part of Europe – a deal still known as the '*Mother Contract*'. The Dutch Republic gradually expanded their trading activities to include other products and to other parts of Europe, and eventually to different parts of the world, with the famous United East India Company (VOC) and West India Company (WIC). The Dutch Republic became the world's main trade society, the VOC the world's largest commercial company and Amsterdam the most important city[3].

### *Leaving the feudal system behind*

The Dutch were the first to leave the feudal system behind and in 1581 they formed a Republic with a written constitution[4]. It was an unprecedented step and a wonder to many people, who asked themselves the question (as formulated by historian Charles Wilson): 'How could a motley collection of tradesmen, salt dealers, fishermen and tallow chandlers hope to govern themselves without royal or even noble guidance?' The provinces were united in The Republic of the Seven United Netherlands, with a president as the country's chief – then named the *Grand Pensionary*. The most famous Grand Pensionary was Johan de Witt, who (supported by his brother Cornelis) brought the country to the pinnacle of the world. Selecting the Grand Pensionary and other political leaders was not a democratic process, however, as the country's upper class regents made that choice.

The Grand Pensionary and the regents held the Republic's political power, which was separated from the economic power and the judiciary. Merchants held most of the commercial power, while judges became independent from merchants and politicians to form a reliable third party for resolving conflicts regarding commercial contracts, for example. The split of political, economic and legal powers was a societal novelty, one replicated thereafter by many other countries, and is still the basis for many societies.

### *Citizenship*

Citizenship in the Netherlands of the 17th century was unique. It was achieved either through heritage or financial transaction and bestowed a person with the right to become a member of communities: a guild, a brotherhood, a district or a neighbourhood, for example. Only citizens were allowed to become a member of the city government. One important condition of citizenship was that the person had to be settled and residing in the city, another was 'honourable public behaviour'. People from outside the city or those without a permanent residence had no influence. Citizenship was a combination of rights (solidarity) and duties (loyalty), with the result that citizens were very much involved in the local community. One important duty was the obligation to defend the city as a member of the citizen force, then called the 'Night Watch'[5]. Over time, the number of duties and obligations increased and were also expected from other social groups, which increased societal inclusivity.

Just how unique Dutch citizenship was has been described by Christian Von Krockow in his analysis of Dutch and German societies. Due to a number of wars, Germany did not have a citizen-based society in the 17th century. Instead, it was an authoritarian state. Von Krockow observed[6]: 'Generations of dutifulness made people helpless and incapable of resistance when the State wasn't led decently but by criminals. Or worse: duty as a surrogate religion wore the armour of a clear conscience. Because even those who operated the Holocaust machine could insist they were obeying orders and just doing their job, their duty.'

### *Market economy*

Trade had become the most important economic activity, yet the Dutch Republic was not free of agrarian production. Farmers started to specialise in a limited number of agriproducts that could be brought to the market more efficiently, with the aim of maximising profits from their operation. Demand and supply became the key concept and delivering what the market wanted the main economic driver. The Republic became a market economy and the discipline of the market made its presence felt everywhere. The Dutch commercial infrastructure also developed rapidly, with, for example, the founding of the Amsterdam Exchange Bank which helped the Republic to become the main financial and commodity market in the world. It facilitated the supply of cheap capital and the option for investors to take a small share in a trading venture and so spread their investments in small amounts over a number of projects. The Dutch trading system became a clearinghouse for a wide range of commodities and, as a result, Amsterdam became the most important city in the world.

The Dutch Republic was growing fast because it acted fast and revamped the societal structure very quickly, but also because the competing larger countries reacted slowly. While Spanish ships were still focused on 'collecting' gold and other precious resources to enrich the country's reserves, Great Britain slowly learned from the Dutch and developed as a competing trade nation. The ships of the Dutch Republic and Great Britain sailed the globe looking for new trading opportunities and the competing nations created global empires with colonies on all continents. The Dutch merchant fleet numbered over 2,000 sea-going ships (more than Great Britain and France combined) and many more smaller coasters. The Dutch ships were especially designed to carry bulk cargo and the efficiency of the ship design was much greater because the ships' smaller crews enabled them to charge lower freight rates than their competitors. In other words, innovation in ship design helped the Dutch to gain and sustain world dominance in the trade market. The Dutch were responsible for setting up maritime trade routes to the Iberian Peninsula, Baltic Sea, White Sea, Asia, Africa and the western hemisphere. Globalisation had been invented.

The Dutch Republic was the world's dominant trader, which was remarkable as the Netherlands had a population of only 2.5 million people at the time, far smaller than that of Great Britain or any other leading country. In their bid for a greater global market share, the Dutch Republic and Great Britain fought many battles and wars, including trade wars. In one of these trade wars, the British banned the export of unfinished cloths in 1614 and in return the Dutch banned the import of finished cloths from England. But the British needed the Dutch trading network, while the Dutch needed large markets for their products outside the borders of the Republic. As a result, the Dutch and British textile activities started to intertwine, which had major consequences later on.

## Society 3.0: The Industrial Society

The Dutch Republic inspired other societies to separate their economic, political and legal powers, develop a new societal system, financial system and market economy, and to innovate processes for greater efficiency. However, the production processes remained largely unchanged and continued to use manpower, horsepower, water and wind as the main means of production. With the arrival of the 'Spinning Jenny' as the world's first steam-powered machine (1764) a new era began, one that would lead to industrial societies. An era of mass production, mass consumption and powerful, globally-operating private organisations.

Henry Ford, well-known for his automobiles ('in any colour, so long as it is black') and his notable public aphorisms, once said: 'A prosperous economy requires that workers be able to buy the products that they produce.'[7] He walked the talk by paying his employees well, so that they could buy a car. With this observation, Ford explained in a nut shell the huge economic success of the industrial economy. After buying a car, Ford's employees used the rest of their pay cheque to buy a refrigerator, washing machine, air-conditioning and many more products and services. Producing washing machines and refrigerators also required human labour, whose pay cheques were also used to acquire products and services. This is the economic engine of the industrial society: more people with an income results in more consumption and spending, which results in more demand for labour, which results in more people with an income. Economic growth became a societal objective and for the first time in the history of mankind full employment became an achievable goal. With economic growth, more people became wealthy, sometimes even extremely wealthy, and the demand for capital exploded.

The economic interests of workers and investors in an industrial society are fundamentally the same: both want economic growth. Yet their interests differ when it comes to dividing the jointly created wealth. Workers want higher salaries and more benefits, investors more profits and a higher return on investments. This wealth distribution issue, along the lines of Adam Smith's economic growth factors of labour and capital, became the main topic of interest among writers, economists and politicians in the nineteenth and twentieth centuries. While the governance systems of industrial societies often differ – republics and monarchies, democracies and autocracies – industrial economic systems need to balance the two growth factors of labour and capital. In democratic societies, political parties represent the public's relative preferences in terms of these two factors, with labour on the left side of the balance (e.g. the Labour Party in the UK) and capital on the right side (e.g. the Tories). Apart from differences in religious and ethical perspectives and all kinds of specifically local societal issues, the left-sided parties emphasise the economic importance of the worker's buying power and advocate that created value be more or less equally shared, while right-sided parties emphasise the trickle-down mechanism of investors' higher profits and argue that rewards should be related to relative added value. By voting for political parties or their representatives, civilians provide a mandate to lead and govern the nation-state along the lines of labour and capital. Some democratic states employ a direct democracy in which people can vote for presidential candidates, such as in the United States, while in indirect democracies, such as the Netherlands, people vote for political parties, not individuals.

Economically, the industrial society has been a huge success. Whereas in previous societal structures, having a decent income was the privilege of the elite, in the industrial society it became increasingly achievable for most of the population. Mass consumption stimulated the demand for products, with increased employment as a result. In the industrial economy, the gross national product (GDP) exploded, which resulted in a sharp increase in the prosperity of the human population.

The result of high economic growth was an increasing number of companies and many of these companies became larger, richer and more powerful. Their economic power effectuated greater influence in the political arena, stressing the importance of free markets and the positive effects of economic growth on employment and prosperity. This mobilised societal counterforces, articulating the need for a more equal distribution of the created economic value (Piketty, 2014). Tensions rose between the interests of companies and investors (capital: right) and employees (labour: left). Public services such as education and health care became government responsibilities and, consequently, governments expanded – just like industrial enterprises.

### *Globalisation*

Over time, industrial enterprises expanded their activities beyond their country's borders in the pursuit of international sales and/or lower production costs. These enterprises evolved to become multinational companies that became large and powerful organisations with, in many cases, hundreds of thousands of employees. A new arena emerged at the global level, with multinationals aiming at realising the objectives of their shareholders and national representatives. For political leaders of these countries – also called nation-states – the country's global competitive position became more important, as well as the attractiveness of their business climate for multinationals. The competitive position of small countries vis-à-vis multinational enterprises deteriorated, which gave rise to larger and more powerful regional country associations, such as the European Union.

**During the globalisation wave, another development took off: the emergence of digital technologies. The combination of globalisation and digitalisation is currently changing societies fundamentally.**

***Notes***

1 The world's oldest known man-made structure is Göbekli Tepe (meaning Potbelly Hill) in Turkey. It is a temple built from massive carved stones around 11,000 years old, crafted and constructed by people who had not yet developed metal tools. The megaliths predate Stonehenge by some 6,000 years.

2 Also dubbed Mercantilism

3 In his 2019 book ***Hydropolitics: cooperation and conflict on seven seas*** (in Dutch), Haroon Sheikh investigated the new order that is emerging on the world's seas and oceans.

4 San Marino is the world's oldest republic. According to historians, San Marino declared itself independent from the Roman Empire somewhere between the fourth and eighth century. According to official San Marino information, the city-sized state was founded in 301 AD by a skilled builder called Saint Marinus. Its written constitution was adopted on October 8, 1600, while the nation was recognised by Napoleon's France in 1797 and by other European nations at the 1815 Congress of Vienna.

5 The most famous Dutch painting and one of the world's most important works of art is De Nachtwacht (The Night Watch), painted by Rembrandt Van Rijn (1606-1669).

6 The 'Huizinga Lezing' (Huizinga Lecture) of 1993. In Van Lotringen, 2018: 55.

7 Henry Ford and Samuel Crowther, 1926.

# SOCIETY 4.0 - THE DIGITAL WAVE

# 3

Industrial societies are territory-related nation-states that enable industrial organisations to create wealth for the nation's civilians by means of mass production. All aspects of society support industrial production, including the financial and legal systems, education, health care, housing, the monetary system and public infrastructure, among many other elements. In industrial societies, wealth is distributed among shareholders, the employees of private and public organisations and other citizens, which creates the nation's well-being. As a result, the number of poor people in industrial societies changed from the majority to a minority and full employment became a reachable objective.

Industrial societies have been developing in waves related to available technologies and resources: industrial revolutions. The *First Industrial Revolution* was driven by the steam engine, invented by Jerónimo de Ayanz y Beaumont and initially used for the mass production of textile, as with James Hargreaves' *Spinning Jenny* (1764), the world's first machine. It replaced the traditional power sources of human power, horses, windmills and watermills. The *Second Industrial Revolution* replaced steam engines with combustion engines, using steel rather than wood and oil rather than steam as the main resources. Electricity was used for lighting and powering appliances, assembly lines, railroad systems and many other applications. Society became increasingly materialistic, as people spent more and more of their income on machines that made life more comfortable, such as washing machines, refrigerators and cars.

In 2011, Jeremy Rifkin introduced the term '*Third Industrial Revolution*' for process automation driven by IT and computer technology. This third industrial wave arguably started in 1971 with the first commercially available microprocessor, the Intel 4004. Digital technologies led to an infrastructure of computers, software and algorithms and applications such as social networks, big data, block chains, cryptocurrencies, Internet of Things and virtual and augmented reality. Many analogous mechanical products and services were replaced by digital alternatives, such as the digital camera. New materials, like carbon fibre, started to replace steel and aluminium.

## Vertical application of digital technologies

While digital technologies became a new additional sector in the 'Third Industrial Revolution' (*horizontally added to the economy*), digital technologies soon started to impact and change all sectors. Digital technologies were *vertically* applied in industrial companies, trading companies and agriculture. Gradually, digital technologies and digital companies changed the face of the economy and the economic value generated by digital activities overtook the value generated by industrial activities. The consequence was that the digital wave became an additional societal wave – on top of the industrial, trade and agricultural waves. Business models and value chains were fundamentally redesigned, and so most industries and public services became disrupted by these technologies and applications. Existing companies were faced with new competitors armed with digital business models, such as Uber (taxis), Airbnb (hotels) and Booking.com (travel).

The impact of the large number of digital technologies and innovations becomes visible in a taxonomy that correlates the technologies with the societal and economic consequences. The taxonomy is based on the societal waves in the previous chapter – the agrarian society, the trade society and the industrial society – to which the digital society is added. Correlating digital technologies with economic activities that developed during different societal waves provides an overview of the fundamental consequences of digital technologies and their applications.

As in the Industrial Revolution, the Digital Revolution has come in a series of waves. The taxonomy currently consists of two different waves: the digital wave (4.1) and the artificial intelligence wave (4.2)[1].

## Digital wave 4.1: The societal consequences

The digital wave 4.1 consists of three technologies that lead to digital transformation of businesses and organisations (vertically).

*Big Data*: Digital companies like Google and Facebook collect large amounts of data on individuals and organisations. Algorithms create value by clustering and connecting data and finding patterns. The digital companies then sell this valuable data, mainly for advertising purposes. Big data is also used to create detailed risk profiles (e.g. for insurance companies). In retail, big data helps firms to understand consumer needs, boost sales through upsell- and cross-sell efforts and optimise purchasing activities.

*Internet (of Things)*: By using sensors, GPS navigation, cameras and other technologies, 'things' are able to communicate without human interference. An example is Ocado's logistical centre in Andover, England. In this facility, which is the size of six football fields, dozens of robots move at speeds of up to 6 m/s on self-calculated routes to collect articles.

*Virtual Reality/Augmented Reality*: VR/AR software was first developed in the military, became mature and professional in the gaming industry and is currently used in many business applications, such as architecture and training. For example, VR/AR software for training heart surgeons has been replacing practicing on pigs' hearts.

**The digital wave 4.1**

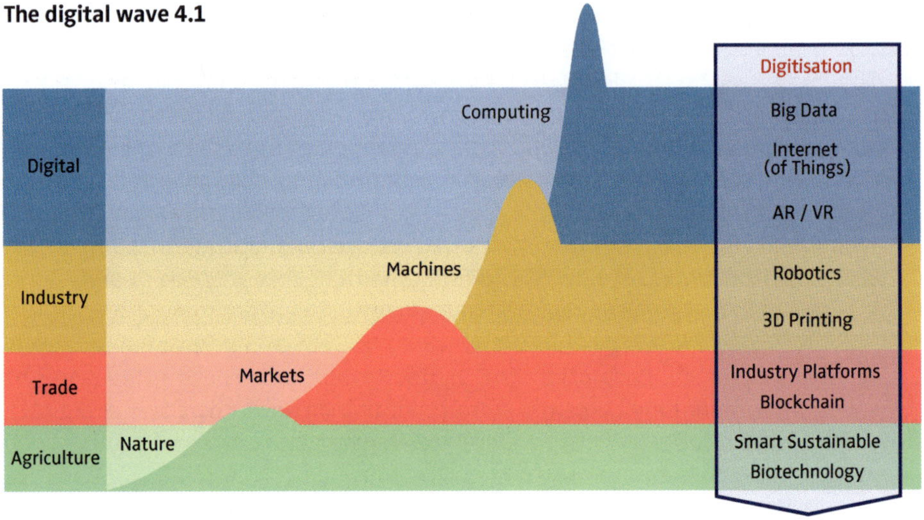


*Figure 3.1: Taxonomy Digital Wave 4.1*

### *Combining digital technologies with machines*

*Robotics*: Efforts to embed robotics in industrial production have been on-going for decades. However, in combination with digital technologies, robots are now achieving high levels of advancement. One advanced robot in particular has captured the attention of many: Atlas, developed by Boston Dynamics. Atlas is shaped like a human body: two legs, two arms and a torso. Atlas is able to walk, run, do back flips and navigate soft surfaces like fresh snow – in other words, basically every physical action humans are capable of. However, the capabilities of Atlas can also be duplicated in other robots, which is a huge advantage over humans, who are not able to duplicate their capabilities in other humans. Each human being has to develop their own knowledge, capabilities and skills. In addition, robots work 24/7 because they do not sleep, take vacations or become ill. As a result, over time, robots will gradually replace human labour.

*3D Printing*: Mass production is the core of industrial production. Economies of scale reduce the cost price per unit and the demand for the product increases. A large number of companies are involved in matching supply and demand, including value system partners such as transportation and shipping companies, distribution, wholesale and retail. 3D printing technology will change that value system and reduce the number of value system partners. The number of products that are being replaced by 3D printing is increasing; for example, 3D printing of houses, ships' propellors and organic materials like skin and bone.

### *Combining digital technologies with markets*

*Industry Platforms*: Another important application of digital technologies is industry platforms. The digital business models of platform organisations like Uber and Airbnb have already revolutionised many industries, and many others will follow. Industry platforms bring together the demand for and supply of products and services. For example, Uber matches demand and supply in transportation and Airbnb does the same for accommodation. These digital business models compete for customers with the traditional models of taxis and hotels.

*Blockchains*: A blockchain is a digital ledger of information in a value chain. When industry players share the digital ledger of an industry they all have access to the most actual and correct information. Producers of sustainable chocolate, for example, benefit from the transparency on upstream steps in the value chain and being able to live up to their promises. Corrupted ledger information can also be easily repaired by reverting to previous versions.

Blockchains can be used as the information basis of economic communities by creating decentralised local economies. For example, by using the rooftops of houses to generate solar energy, the production of energy can be decentralised and the energy can be traded or bartered with other locally produced products and services, such as fruit and vegetables. Information on the relative value of traded products and services is represented in digital value units – also called cryptocurrencies.

### *Combining digital technologies with nature*

*Biotechnology*: For thousands of years, humans' relationship with nature has been changing. To feed an ever-increasing population, and using advanced technological knowledge, humans have started manipulating the cultivation of vegetables and the breeding of animals in order to mass-produce food. In the 21st century, biotechnology – the genetic engineering of living organisms or their components – expanded to include genomics, immunology and recombinant gene technology. New advancements promise future production of cultured meat, an in vitro culture of animal cells, which will eventually replace slaughtered animals.

## Artificial intelligence wave 4.2: The societal consequences

In 1996, World Chess Champion Gary Kasparov lost a chess game to Deep Blue, an IBM chess computer equipped with the first generation of artificial intelligence. This moment marked the beginning of a new era, one in which humans are no longer the most intelligent creatures on earth.

The consequences of artificial intelligence are different from the digital technologies in the first wave (4.1). While digital technologies replace physical work, artificial intelligence replaces the human brain. In addition, the human brain can be 'upgraded' with artificial intelligence, and combinations of robots and artificial intelligence may well lead to forms of artificial life.

**The digital wave 4.2**

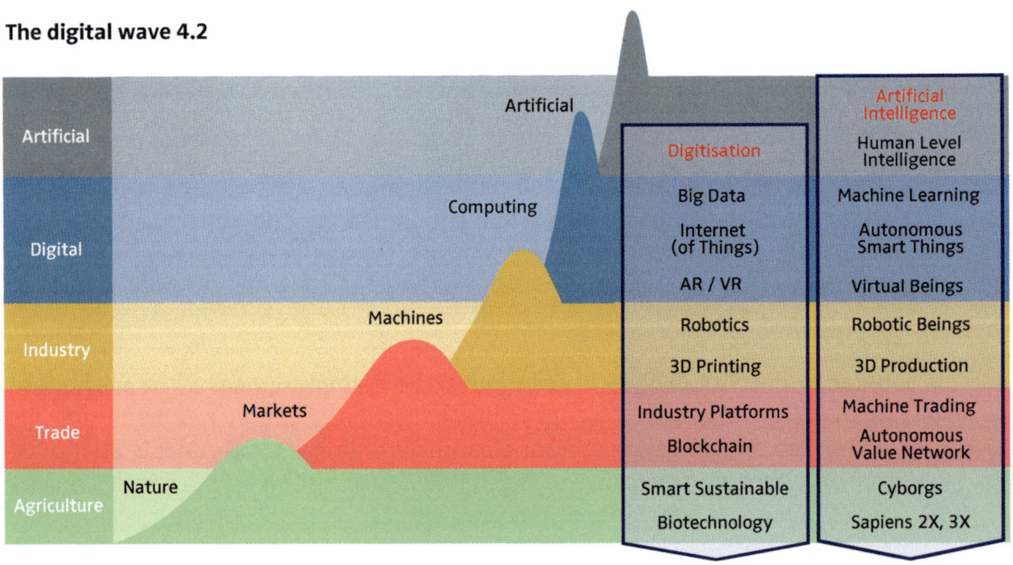


*Figure 3.2: Taxonomy Digital Wave 4.2*

Deep Blue was an early version of what is currently dubbed 'rule-based AI': it was armed with the rules of chess and information on previous chess games. It had learned to play chess better and faster and without making mistakes (supervised learning). Later, humans were also beaten by rule-based AI in GO and Jeopardy.

However, rule-based intelligence is not the essence of human intelligence. What makes humans intelligent is the ability to discover unknown patterns, also called 'pattern recognition'. 'Pattern-based AI', based on 'unsupervised learning', would be very difficult to distinguish from human intelligence. Ray Kurzweil, CTO at Google, expects that in 2029 AI will have achieved a human level of intelligence 'and pass a valid Turing test'. From that point on it will be impossible to distinguish between human and artificial intelligence without physical human presence.

### *Combining artificial intelligence with computing*

*Machine learning*: Combining artificial intelligence with digital technologies leads to machine learning that adds intelligence to datasets without human interference. Early examples are Watson in health and Ross in legal. Watson and Ross are able to diagnose and propose solutions, just like medical and legal professionals. But machine learning is faster and makes fewer mistakes than human professionals. As a result, machine learning is changing the professional domain. Professionals such as medics, lawyers and accountants will have to acquire the skills needed to cooperate with machine learning systems and learn how to combine their 'human touch' with machine learning knowledge.

*Virtual beings*: By combining virtual reality, big data and artificial intelligence, the boundaries between real and virtual 'humans' are being blurred. In China, for example, an 'artificial intelligent anchor' reads the daily news. This news anchor is a hologram, designed on the basis of a popular Chinese news anchor, and reads news that is selected by intelligent algorithms (and approved by the Communist Party). The facial expressions while reading are very human. Over time, it will even become possible to have a virtual version of yourself.

### *Combining artificial intelligence with machines*

*Robotic beings*: Combining robots with artificial intelligence may lead to inorganic life species that can imitate any form of life, including humans. The first robotic human-like being was Sophia, who received global attention when granted citizenship by Saudi Arabia. By changing the rubber face, it is possible to create mirror versions of famous people like Albert Einstein. The intelligence of Sophia does not yet match human intelligence, but this will probably be achieved within a few years.

### *Combining artificial intelligence with markets*

On stock markets and other exchanges, intelligent algorithms have taken over (at least partly) from human traders. In *Machine trading*, also called *Algorithmic trading*, *Electronic trading* and *Automated trading*, machines process and analyse large amounts of data and buy and sell shares or resources on the basis of algorithms. Machine trading is used by investment banks, pension funds, mutual funds and hedge funds, as machines are able to trade faster than human traders. According to Bigiotti & Navarra (2018)[2], over 80% of trading in the FOREX market in 2016 was performed by machines rather than humans. One widely used application is 'high-frequency trading' (HFC), which is characterised by high turnover and high order-to-trade ratios (Lemke & Lins, 2015-16)[3]. With HFC, computers make decisions based on information that is received electronically and before human traders can process the information.

### *Combining artificial intelligence with nature*

*Sapiens 2.X*: Biotechnology is not only applicable to plants and animals but also to humans. One prominent example is the scientific discovery by microbiologists Emmanuelle Charpentier and Jennifer Doudna of the CRISPR-Cas9 technology, a new technology that can be used to modify human DNA. This genetic manipulation method makes it possible to 'cut out' hereditary diseases, such as HIV, cystic fibrosis, cancer and Alzheimer's. The first public application of the technology occurred in China, where the Chinese scientist He Jiankui used it to cut out HIV from an infected sperm donor. After fertilising a woman with the sperm, the twin sisters Lulu and Nana were born healthy.

*Sapiens 3.X*: Using 'brain-computer interfaces' (BCI) computers will be directly connected with human brains. This technology is developing fast and the expectation of many is that human intelligence and artificial intelligence will soon be merging into so-called cyber-physical systems. Elon Musk, founder of the new company Neuralink that connects computers with human brains, even believes that developing cyber-physical systems is crucial if mankind wants to be able to keep up with the intelligent artificial creatures of the future.

***Notes***

[1] A frequently asked question is what the driver of the third wave will be. Several technologies have the potential to form a new wave, but the most likely candidate is quantum computing. Given that there are so many uncertainties, including the global consequences of the corona 'pandemic', I will not discuss this in this book.

[2] Bigiotti, Alessandro and Alfredo Navarra, 'Optimizing Automated Trading Systems', ***Advances in Intelligent Systems and Computing***, Springer International Publishing, October 19. 2018, pp. 254–261.

[3] Lemke, Thomas. P. and Gerald T. Lins (ed.), ***Soft Dollars and Other Trading Activities***, Thomson West, 2015–2016.

# THE FOURTH SOCIETAL REVOLUTION OR 'JUST' A FOURTH *INDUSTRIAL* REVOLUTION?

# 4

Digital technologies are changing our society and economy at least as fundamentally as machines changed societies and economies in the industrial revolution. Digital technologies do not just add another industry to the economy, they change the whole society and economy, a process referred to as 'digital transformation' or 'the digital revolution'. The beginning of the digitalisation wave was quite simple and visible: email messages began to replace physical mail and the postman and webshops began to cannibalise retail outlets. These industries and companies were quickly hit by the digitalisation wave, but for many others it took a lot longer and in some cases this fundamental change is only being felt now, for example in legal and governmental systems. On the current electronic highway you will still find racing cars and horse-drawn carriages.

The digital wave is often dubbed the '*Fourth Industrial Revolution*'. This term was first introduced by Klaus Schwab in a 2015 article in *Foreign Affairs*: 'The Fourth Industrial Revolution, What It Means and How to Respond'. The technological drivers of his fourth wave coincide roughly with those in Rifkin's 'Third Industrial Revolution': artificial intelligence, robotics, the Internet of Things, autonomous vehicles, 3D printing, nanotechnology, biotechnology, materials science, energy storage and quantum computing. The fourth industrial wave has also been dubbed Industry 4.0, the Industrial Internet (General Electric), the Internet of Everything (Cisco), Internet 4.0 and 'the Industrial Internet of Things' (Gilchrist, 2016).

The popularity of the term '*Fourth Industrial Revolution*' really took off at the World Economic Forum Annual Meeting in 2016 in Davos, Switzerland. At this event, Klaus Schwab, founder and executive chairman of the World Economic Forum, announced the opening of its *Centre for the Fourth Industrial Revolution* in San Francisco on October 10, 2016. Schwab expected the fourth industrial wave to be marked by 'breakthroughs in emerging technologies in fields such as robotics, artificial intelligence, nanotechnology, quantum computing, biotechnology, the internet of things, the industrial internet of things (IIoT), decentralised consensus, fifth-generation wireless technologies (5G), 3D printing and fully autonomous vehicles' (Schwab, 2016).

## Transforming societies and the global economy

Klaus Schwab also expected that 'technologies would transform societies and the global economy'. Yet the term '*Fourth Industrial Revolution*' assumes that society will remain industrial and that societal structure itself will not change, meaning that the main characteristics of the industrial society remain intact.

This is highly unlikely, however, because of four fundamental developments: economic value distribution, tax evasion consequences, undemocratic decision-making and the strengthened societal factor 'capital'.

## Economic value distribution

In industrial economies, the created economic value is distributed among all stakeholders, including governments and citizens. Whereas in feudal societies (the first societal wave) all created value was captured by the 'one percent elite', in industrial societies a much more equal value distribution took place: the majority of citizens were able to earn a decent income.

From the beginning of the 1970s on, however, a reverse trend became visible. As Figure 4.1 illustrates, in the US the value distribution among the 50 percent of citizens with the lowest income has roughly halved, while the share of the 1 percent elite has doubled. Extrapolation of this trend would mean that the future distribution of created value will resemble that of a feudal society.

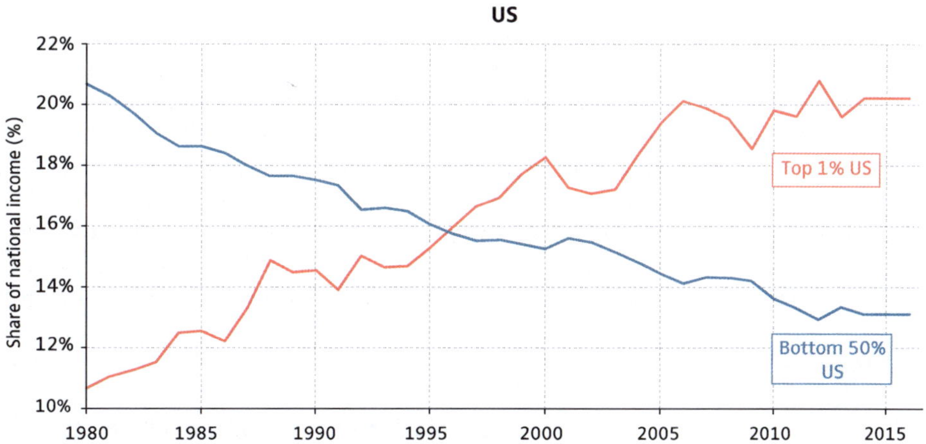


Source: WID.world (2017). See wir2018.wid.world/methodology.html for data series and notes.

In 2016, 12% of national income was received by the top 1% in Western Europe, compared to 20% in the United States. In 1980, 10% of national income was received by the top 1% in Western Europe, compared to 11% in the United States.

*Figure 4.1: Share of US National Income 1980-2015*

## Tax evasion consequences

In an industrial society, economic welfare finances societal well-being. Companies, investment firms and rich individuals pay taxes, by which they contribute to developing and maintaining social facilities such as education and health care. Political representatives determine the different tax categories and rates. This assumes, however, that the fiscal rules for the financial elite are determined on a democratic and fair basis.

However, in recent decades the power balance between some multinationals (corporate-states) and their shareholders on one side and countries (nation-states) on the other has shifted dramatically. The new power balance is visible in the relative amount of taxes being paid and evaded. Because of 'fiscal optimisation' – a fancy term for tax evasion by actively using various constructions to pay less or zero tax – multinationals, their shareholders and rich individuals are now roaming the globe searching for the most attractive corporate and private 'residences'. Some multinationals are behaving increasingly like corporate-states and rich individuals like 'global citizens', a development that is being enabled by a number of countries – 'tax havens' – that offer corporate-states and global citizens an 'attractive business climate'.

And there are many tax havens. In 2017, the European Union began publishing a 'black list' of countries and regions outside of the European Union where authorities do not levy taxes (or at very low rates), are not transparent and disapprove of the battle against tax evasion. The list published on 18 February 2020 lists the following territories as tax havens outside Europe: Fiji, American Samoa, Guam, the American Virgin Islands, Oman, Trinidad and Tobago, Vanuatu and Samoa, Palau, Panama, the Seychelles and – after the exit of Great Britain – the Cayman Islands[1]. Oxfam Novib has added the European countries Cyprus, Ireland, Luxembourg, Malta and the Netherlands (Oxfam Novib, 18 February 2020) to the list of tax havens. In 2019, the international Tax Justice Network (TJN) published a top 10 list of countries that 'do the most to facilitate tax evasion by multinationals and to undermine the global tax system': the British Virgin Islands, Bermuda, Cayman Islands, the Netherlands, Switzerland, Luxembourg, Jersey, Singapore, Bahamas and Hong Kong[2].

The financial loss due to tax evasion activities has been estimated by Oxfam Novib at approximately 100 billion euro per year, money that 'cannot be spent, for example, on health care and education'. This amount could 'provide 2.2 billion people with good basic health care, clean drinking water and sanitary facilities, and the educational budget of the forty-seven poorest countries could be quadrupled.' This situation resembles the relative proportions of the feudal age, but then on a global scale.

## Undemocratic decision-making

In an industrial society, decisions on societal issues such as education, healthcare and the economy are made by means of democratic decision-making processes. For many decades, democratic decision-making has taken place at the local, national or regional level (such as the EU), or combinations of these levels. Increasingly, however, societal issues are transcending traditional geographic borders. Climate change is an example, as are transmittable diseases such as HIV, Ebola, SARS, hepatitis, influenza and coronavirus, which spread more easily due to the international transportation of goods and the increased mobility of people.

Non-governmental organisations (NGOs) have been established to tackle a wide range of global issues, often within the United Nations ecosystem. Independent of national governments, these globally operating NGOs address issues such as protecting human rights and development aid. The number of NGOs has risen from 400 one hundred years ago to over 40,000 today, with a combined budget of $25-30 billion[3]. These organisations have become increasingly important in national and international political decision-making[4] as a consequence of increased globalisation (Risse, 2013, 251[5]).

Democratic decision-making, which is common in industrial societies, does not happen at the global level, however. Corporate-states and NGOs are not democracies, and neither are global citizens or global charities[6]. Possible problematic consequences were already identified in 1995: 'Business and government are organized at the national level. There is a growing need to articulate countervailing visions (...). In the long run, we have to invent the infrastructure so citizens can participate effectively in the democratic management of the global system. Over the next decade, NGOs and their networks are one of the important precursors of an accountable global civil society.'[7]

## Strengthened societal factor 'capital'

Increasingly, the societal factor 'labour' is not balancing out the powerful societal factor 'capital', as digital technologies are replacing (paid) human labour at an ever faster rate. For example, robots and the Internet of Things are replacing physical human labour and Machine Learning and Deep Learning (Artificial Intelligence plus Big Data) are now doing the jobs that many professionals once did. The future of work has become a key scientific field, especially since the publication of '*The Future of Work*' in 2013 by Oxford University scientists Carl Frey and Michael Osborne[8]. In this book, the authors published the results of their research on the amount of paid labour that will be available in the future as a consequence of the large number of digital technologies. Their conclusion that two-thirds of all current labour will 'likely or very likely' vanish in the future is on the high end of most scientists' expectations, but a serious decline in employment is generally expected. This decline cannot be compensated by new work resulting from the digital wave – the main counterargument of critics. Many low-skilled, repetitive tasks are becoming obsolete, while an elite of software architects, designers, engineers, IT specialists, online marketing staff and other highly educated professionals will increasingly become key resources. A crucial consequence of this development is that the strategic societal factor 'labour' will become weaker and the societal factor 'capital' stronger.

***Notes***

1 This list was updated during the EU consultation between European Ministers of Finance on 18 February 2020. Bermuda is not on the list, as there was no agreement.

2 Mark Mansour, 'New ranking reveals corporate tax havens behind breakdown of global corporate tax system; toll of UK's tax war exposed', Tax Justice Network, May 28, 2019.

3 I take the number to be 40,000, but the exact number of NGOs is unknown. For example, as David Lewis writes (Nongovernmental Organizations, Definition and History, Political Science, 2009): 'It is difficult to know precisely how many NGOs there are, because few comprehensive or reliable statistics are kept (...) The United Nations estimates that there were about 35,000 large established NGOs in 2000. Nor are there accurate figures available for the amount of resources that NGOs receive from aid, contracts and private donations. In 2004, it was estimated that NGOs were responsible for about $23 billion of total aid money (...)'.

4 See, for example, Betsill, Michele. M. & Elisabeth Corell. (2001), 'NGO Influence in International Environmental Negotiations: A Framework for Analysis', Global Environmental Politics, 2001 (4): 65-85; Keck, Margaret E. & Kathryn Sikkink, 'Transnational Advocacy Networks in International and Regional Politics', International Social Science Journal, 1999, 51 (159), 89-101; Carpenter, Charli, Sirin Duygulu, Alexander H. Montgomery & Anna Rapp, 'Explaining the Advocacy Agenda: Insights from the Human Security Network', International Organization, 2014, 68(2): 449-470; Risse, Thomas, 'Transnational Actors and World Politics', In: Carlsnaes, Walter, Thomas Risse & Beth Simmons (eds.), Handbook of International Relations. 2013, London: Sage Publications, 426-452).

5 Risse, Thomas, 'Transnational Actors and World Politics', In: Carlsnaes, Walter, Thomas Risse & Beth Simmons (eds.), Handbook of International Relations. 2013, London: Sage Publications, 426-452.

6 See, for example, James A. Paul, 'NGOs and Global Policy-Making', Global Policy Forum, June 2000: '... some accuse NGOs of being structurally undemocratic and unaccountable ... it is true that NGO leaders do not stand for election, they are held accountable by boards of directors, membership bodies, and other constituencies. They also must win voluntary financial support each year from members and donors and cannot rely on legally-enforced taxation as governments do ...'

7 James A. Paul, 'NGOs and Global Policy-Making', ***Global Policy Forum***, June 2000.

8 Frey, Carl B., and Michael Osborne, The Future of Employment: How susceptible are jobs to computerisation?, ***Technological Forecasting and Social Change***, 114: 254-280, 17 September 2013.

# EIGHT KEY ISSUES FOR THE SOCIETAL REVOLUTION

5

Historically, periods in between societies have often been very turbulent. The transition to a new and unknown societal structure requires optimism and perseverance, especially because strong resistance can be expected from societal actors for whom the change is unfavourable. In such times, relatively minor events often work as a catalyst for major societal change – often called the 'butterfly effect'. An extreme example was the famous 'Storming of the Bastille' in France in July 1789. The direct cause was the decision by King Louis XVI to fire the popular finance minister Jacques Necker, but the underlying problems were the economic crisis, increased societal contradictions and discontent over the extravagant lifestyle of the royal family. The Storming appeared to mark the beginning of a better time in which the ugly caterpillar would become a butterfly.

## The Corona butterfly

The term 'butterfly effect' was coined by Edward Lorenz (1963)[1], who observed that a very small change in initial conditions (set in motion by the wings of a butterfly, for example) can have a major effect on the weather, such as the development of a tornado. The weather appeared to be an example of a nonlinear dynamic system, which became the focus of research by scientists in several other domains. Much research has been done, for example, by the renowned Santa Fe Institute on complex adaptive systems. The economy is also a nonlinear dynamic system and as the industrial economic system was already in an existential crisis, any minor event could have led to a fundamental change.

Future historians may well identify the 'Corona crisis' as the catalyst for a system change, a societal revolution that uncovered and addressed fundamental industrial system malfunctions – coronavirus as the end of the capitalist society and the beginning of a new and, hopefully, better society. Although revolutions often lead to uncertainty and pose a threat to the existing holders of power and wealth, they can also be the starting point for social renewal. The Corona crisis may well be the caterpillar of today, marking a transition to the butterfly 'Society 4.0' with the hope of a better future.

In the transition phase between the industrial society and the emerging 'new society' eight fundamental societal issues need to be resolved:

## Issue 1: Rethinking the nation-state concept

With private companies growing ever bigger and more global and nation-states changing slowly and remaining 'national', the power balance between global companies and national governments has been changing rapidly. Since the direct influence of national governments is limited to the geographical borders that were formed as the result of intentional and accidental historical events, political decision makers tend to act in the interest of the voters they represent (e.g. 'America First'). They strive for economic growth and more jobs in order to provide their voters with more income. Global companies, however, serve customers worldwide in the interest of their globally active shareholders. And as national voters are also international customers, governments and companies share an economic interest in having citizens with ample purchasing power. As long as people are wealthy enough to consume products and services, their interests will remain aligned and so they will not revolt against governments or companies.

On the value creation side and the value distribution side, however, the interests of nation-states and global companies do differ. Global companies choose the physical and fiscal location where their products and services are produced and national governments try to seduce companies to locate these value activities in their national territories in order to boost economic growth and employment. Consequently, nation-states are constantly competing with each other to gain the favour of global companies when deciding where to locate their value creating activities.

Global companies are gaining more and more power at the expense of governments and national interests and, without a strong countervailing power, will most likely continue to do so in the future. Corporate-states (including digitech, finance and pharma) will continue to rapidly increase in size (turnover) and power (data), while nation-states will show moderate growth at best. Most nation-states will not be able to catch up with the dominant globalising powers and some of them will form cooperative regional initiatives, such as the European Union and other nation-state alliances, with varying degrees of success, as Brexit has illustrated. The global arena will then consist of large corporate-states and a few large nation-states, such as China, India and the United States, and other alliances of cooperating countries. Most nation-states will become peripheral on the world stage, much more so than today. Since citizens in these peripheral nation-states will have no influence on developments in the global arena, they will be dependent on what a few large nation-states and the large corporate-states decide for them.

## Issue 2: Rethinking the governance of societies

Rising and structural unemployment has a major effect on the income of large groups of citizens and the economic models of societies. But the governance of society needs to be revised as well, as it affects the power balance between capital and labour and therefore the power balance between citizens with and without income. From the perspective of Adam Smith's economic growth factors of capital and labour, a growing power inequality between societal players with and without income will change society's governance model. In democratic countries, 'left-wing' political parties and presidential candidates are struggling with their political positioning. Labour parties are no longer dominant players in the political arena. In the vacuum created by the current political system, new political parties have emerged. In the Netherlands these include the Green Party ('capitalists are destroying the planet'), Democrats, Party for Freedom, Animal Party and lots of small parties that focus primarily on local issues[2]. These parties represent bubbles of social interest groups that cannot be positioned on the left (labour) or right (capital) side of the traditional power balance.

As Adam Smith's societal growth factors of capital and labour are no longer the crucial variables in societal governance, a new governance model for societies needs to be developed. But different societal stakeholders with different interests hold different views on the envisioned outline of a new societal governance model.

## Issue 3: Rethinking world governance

The main organisation for global issues is the United Nations (UN), established after World War II to prevent future wars. This intergovernmental organisation, with 193 member states, aims to maintain international peace and security, develop friendly relations among nations, achieve international cooperation and be a centre for harmonizing the actions of nations. The UN has its headquarters on international territory in New York City, with other main offices in Geneva, Nairobi, Vienna and The Hague. Since the 1970s, the UN's budget for economic and social development programmes has exceeded its spending on peacekeeping and the organisation has also expanded to include a wide variety of global public domains. Currently, the UN has six principal organs: the General Assembly, the Security Council, the Economic and Social Council (ECOSOC), the Trusteeship Council, the International Court of Justice and the UN Secretariat. The UN System includes a multitude of specialised agencies, such as the World Bank Group, the World Health Organisation, the World Food Programme, UNESCO and UNICEF. Additionally, many non-governmental organisations (NGOs) are granted consultative status within the ECOSOC and other agencies in the UN.

Over the past few decades, United Nations agencies and many NGOs have gained more influence on global issues such as the economy, health and energy. For example, economic interests are discussed and aligned at the World Economic Forum[3] (WEF), health care at the World Health Organisation (WHO) and energy at the International Energy Agency (IEA). However, the term NGO is not univocal: there is a wide range of different NGOs. Most NGOs are non-profit organisations that represent public values, yet some NGOs are for-profit corporations (Karns, 2020), such as the Bill and Melinda Gates Foundation and the Rockefeller Foundation.

The term 'non-governmental organisation' was first coined in 1945 when the United Nations (UN) was created (Thomas, 2014). The UN, itself an 'intergovernmental organisation', made it possible for 'certain approved specialised international non-state agencies' – non-governmental organisations – to be awarded observer status at its assemblies and some of its meetings. Later, the term became used more widely. Today, according to the UN, 'any kind of private organisation that is independent of government control can be termed an NGO, provided it is not-for-profit, but not simply an opposition political party' (Thomas, 2014).

NGOs have existed for centuries: in 1910, 130 international groups organised a coordinating body called the 'Union of International Associations'. In 2020 there were over 6,000 officially recognised international NGOs and many more 'unofficial' NGOs. Over 2,000 NGOs are officially accredited by the UN with consultative status and are automatically granted the right to participate in UN-sponsored conferences. Since the 1970s in particular, the number of international, national and local NGOs has been exploding. International NGOs have been created to address specific issues such as human rights, women's rights and environmental protection and have become important actors in world affairs within UN agencies and forums. The strong growth of international NGOs is the result of many different factors, including the globalisation of companies, increasing prominence of transnational issues, growth in UN-sponsored global conferences, information and communication technology (ICT) and the spread of democracy (Karns, 2020). Most NGOs do great work, but the large number of NGOs and their diversity make it difficult for them to develop a coordinated approach to many issues.

While in the industrial society aligning the interests of companies with public values has mainly taken place at the national or regional level, the new global arena requires alignment mechanisms at the global level. This raises an important governance issue: how can public values be represented in supranational or inter-governmental governance organisations? Citizens are not able to elect representatives to express their preferences on key issues. There is no democratic feedback system in place at the global level.

## Issue 4: Rethinking industrial capitalism

Economically, capitalism has been a phenomenal success. The world economy grew six-fold between 1000 and 1820 and the income of individuals rose by 50 percent, while between 1820 and 1998 the economy grew fifty-fold and the income of individuals showed a nine-fold increase on average, and in Japan even thirty-one-fold. In industrial capitalism, production and most of the inputs and outputs of production are supplied through the market and are negotiable, such as wages, production costs, sales and profits. The standard explanation of the success of capitalism refers to Adam Smith's invisible hand in *An Inquiry into the Nature and Causes of the Wealth of Nations* (1776): free and competitive markets are efficient because resources are not wasted. One condition for a free and competitive market to be effective is the existence of competition. In most countries, governments control the rules and conditions under which companies have to operate, such as competition laws that prohibit monopolies and cartels, following on from the Sherman Antitrust Act in 1890.

As multinational companies went about globalising production, sales and value chains, most countries had different legislation for many relevant factors, such as import and export conditions, tariffs and taxation. Multinationals had to organise, coordinate and align multiple activities between dozens and sometimes hundreds of countries. This complex and suboptimal situation resulted in discussions between global companies and governments on free economic zones and trade agreements, such as the North American Free Trade Agreement (NAFTA) in 1994. Among the key elements of these agreements were dispute resolution mechanisms and legislation.

The changing power balance between companies and countries became visible in negotiations on the Comprehensive Economic and Trade Agreement (CETA), a free trade agreement between Canada and the European Union. CETA was launched at the May 2009 EU–Canada Summit in Prague with the aim of 'eliminating trade and investment barriers between the two territories' and removing 98 percent of the pre-existing tariffs between Canada and the European Union. The negotiations were concluded in August 2014, approved by the European Parliament on 15 February 2017 and ratified by the 28 EU member countries in the following years. CETA received strong criticism, both in European countries and in Canada, particularly in relation to the dispute resolution sections 3 and 4 of the agreement.

Disputes can arise when a company from one country invests in another country – both of which have agreed to the CETA treaty – and the host state violates rights under the treaty. The investor may then bring the issue to an arbitral tribunal for resolution. In the CETA agreement, the legal instrument for dispute resolution is the ISDS (Investor-State Dispute Settlements). ISDS is an instrument of public international law and it covers a number of other international investment and trade treaties as well, such as the NAFTA, CPTPP and the Energy Charter Treaty. It allows investors to sue host country governments (including provincial, state or municipal governments) for any government action that violates the 'legitimate expectations' of companies or investors.

Several cases have already been settled. For example, Lone Pine Resources Inc. sued the Canadian government for more than $250 million under the provisions of NAFTA because a natural gas exploration permit for deposits beneath the St. Lawrence River had been cancelled. The claim was based on 'the loss of a valuable right ... without due process, without compensation and with no recognizable public purpose'[4]. In another case, the pharmaceutical company Eli Lilly presented a 500 million US dollar claim against the government of Canada regarding drug patent legislation[5]. The number of known cases reached over 500 in 2012. Of these, 244 were settled, of which approximately 42% were decided in favour of the host state and approximately 31% in favour of the investor. Approximately 27% of the cases were settled out of court[6]. ISDS dissuades governments from even thinking about passing regulations that might lead to a lawsuit.

CETA[7] provides investment protection and guarantees 'fair and equitable treatment and full protection and security' to foreign investors. Corporations can sue national governments for billions of dollars if they believe that the government's policies have a negative impact on their investments. The protection is one-sided: states cannot sue companies in these investor-state arbitrations. This level of parallel justice is new for transatlantic trade and investment and it empowers companies to circumvent national and European legal systems and impede governments in parallel tribunals in their attempts to, for example, protect public interests or the environment. The one-sided character of CETA has been described by Corporate Europe Observatory's trade campaigner Pia Eberhardt as 'VIP rights for corporations which can thwart government efforts to protect people and the environment, and provide access to billions of taxpayer money'[8].

Governments provide the infrastructure for markets to function, such as issuing funds, providing public utilities and enforcing contracts. Often, governments control other crucial public infrastructure too, such as electricity, cable and communication, without which society could not function, and regulate standards of service in health care, social security and education. However, corporate-states have become much more powerful vis-à-vis governments and crucial elements of public infrastructure, such as energy and cable, have been privatised (often dubbed 'neo-liberalism'). In addition, the new public digital infrastructures of social networking – crucial to a well-functioning society – are all privately owned by the world's largest companies: Facebook, Google, LinkedIn, Microsoft and Apple. The objective of these companies is to maximise shareholder value, not public values.

## Issue 5: Rethinking income distribution

One key characteristic of industrial societies is that employment is an achievable objective for the majority of people, thereby providing them with an income. Compared with previous societal waves, in industrial societies wealth is distributed more evenly over the population. Private wealth is not just for the 'happy one percent'. This is illustrated by the international differences between countries on how income is distributed over citizen groups, measured in terms of the percentage of the share of national income that is distributed over the country's top 10%. In industrialised countries in Western Europe and the USA, wealth distribution across the 10% richest people is *below* 50 percent, while in other countries and regions wealth distribution is *over* 50 percent (Figure 5.1).

The social impact of income distribution has been a topic of debate since Plato's *Republic*, written more than 2,300 years ago. Plato wrote that when a society is ruled by its elites it: '... should of necessity be not one, but two, a city of the rich and a city of the poor, dwelling together, and always plotting against one another.'

The impact of inequality on economic growth has been studied by Richard B. Freeman, who argues that inequality is good for growth – up to a certain point. After this point, rising inequality means falling growth: 'The few people with the skills or background to compete for the top jobs work hard, while everyone else coasts because they have little or no chance of reaching the top.' Freeman makes a case for 'optimal inequality' or, what some have called, 'just-right inequality' – not too little, not too much (OECD, 2015). Studies have found strong evidence that inequality leads to health and social problems' (MacInnes et al., 2015).

The consequences of inequality are also influenced by the 'shape' of inequality, i.e. whether there is a rich elite and everyone else, as in feudal societies, or with small numbers of rich and poor and a large middle class, as in industrial societies. The inequality shape affects the way different income groups behave and how these groups interact. As Sarah Voitchovski (2009) points out: 'If inequality 'squeezes' the middle class it may reduce the demand for goods and services, while the rich may use their economic power to lobby against policies that don't serve their needs, for example in public health ...'

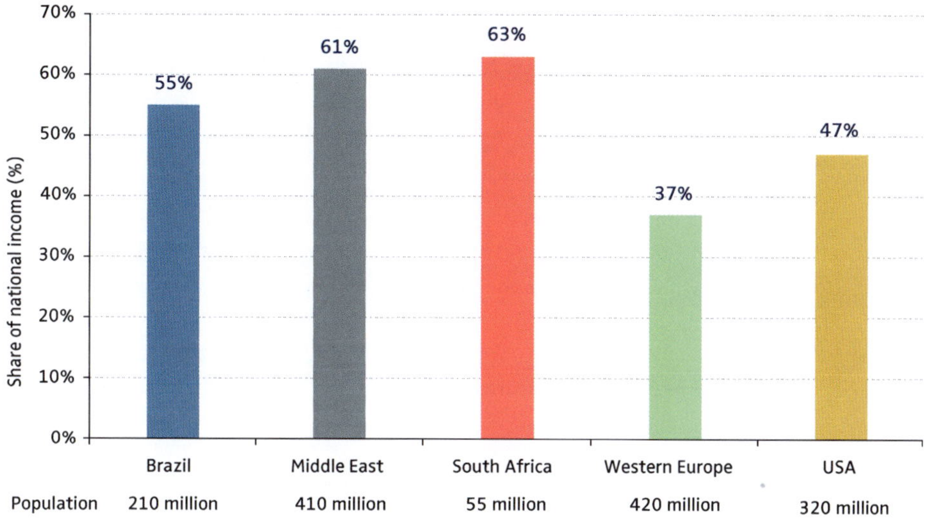


Source: WID.world (2017). See wir2018.wid.world/methodology.html for data series and notes.
In 2016, 61% of national income was received by the top 10% in the Middle East.

*Figure 5.1: Top 10% national income share in Brazil, the Middle East, South Africa and other countries; 2012–2016*

Going back in time, the income share of the top 1 percent in Germany between 1871 and 1914 (Figure 5.2) had significant societal consequences. The two time periods with a sharp increase in the elite's income were between 1910 and 1914 and between 1930 and 1940. The First World War started in 1914 and ended in 1918, while the Second World War started in 1939 and ended in 1945.

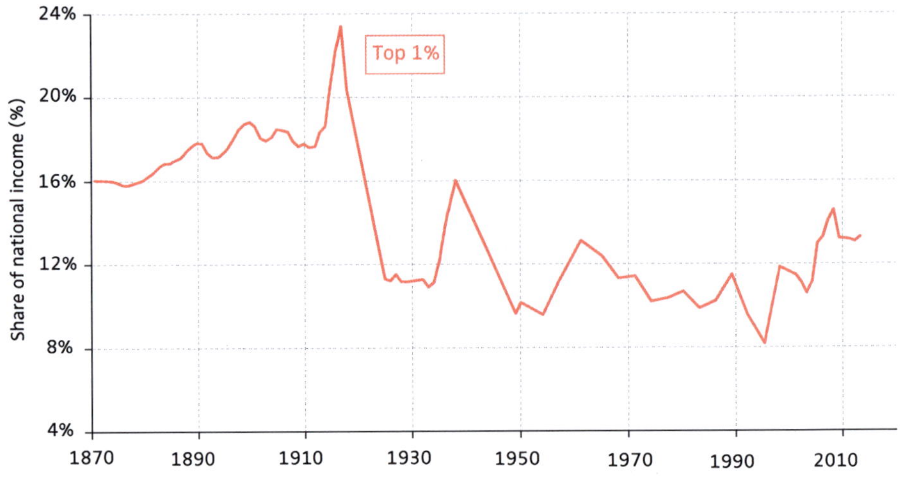


Source: Bartels (2017) See wir 2018.wid.world/methodology.html for data series and notes.
In 2013, the top 1%'s national income share was 13%

*Figure 5.2: Top 1% income share in Germany 1871-2013*

When taking a closer look at the development of wealth distribution in France over more than 200 years (between 1800 and 2014), three separate periods of income distribution can be distinguished. The first period was between 1800 and 1914, the second between 1914 and 1984 and the third from 1984 to the present day. The French society fundamentally changed with the First World War (1914) when the industrialising economy started to change the societal structure. From 1914 on, the share of the top 10% gradually dropped, while the percentage of the middle 40% rose, with the bottom 50% showing moderate growth (Figure 5.3).

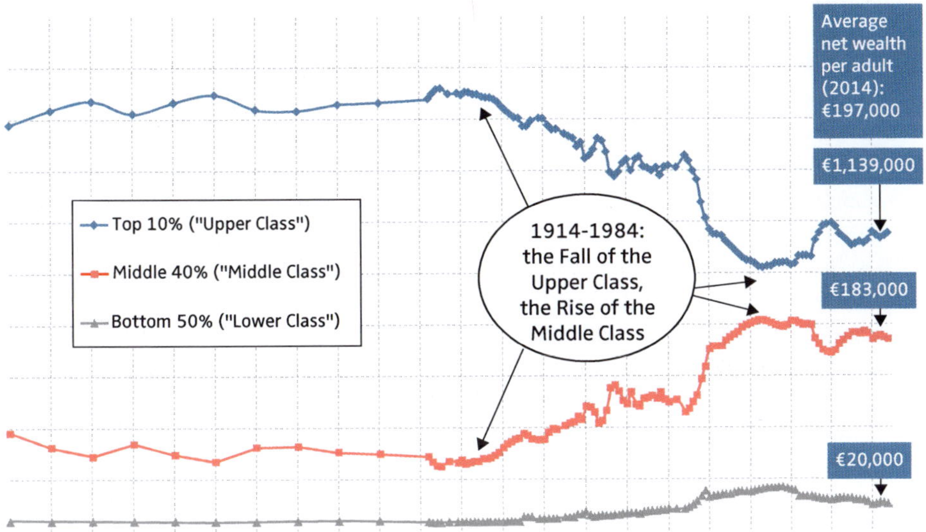


*Figure 5.3: Income distribution in France between 1800 and 2014*

Source: 'Accounting for Wealth Inequality Dynamics: Methods, Estimates and Simulations for France (1800-2014)'; 2016/5 WID.world Working paper.

The trend towards more equal wealth distribution in France ended in the early 1980s, as Figure 5.3 shows, marking the beginning of a new period of inequality in which the top wealth holders are almost exclusively the top capital earners and comprise very few of the top labour earners. In the same period, the importance of the middle class remained more or less stable: from a 68 percent share of national income to 67 percent.

The same trend can be observed in other industrialised countries, such as the United States, as shown in Figure 4.1. Between 1980 and 2015 the share of national income of the top 1% almost doubled from around 11 percent in 1980 to over 20 percent, while the share of the bottom 50 percent dropped from 21 percent in 1980 to 13 percent in 2015. The trend towards more inequality matches the hypothesis of Piketty (2014) that 'the world today is returning towards "patrimonial capitalism", in which much of the economy is dominated by inherited wealth: the power of this economic class is increasing, threatening to create an oligarchy.'

## Issue 6: Rethinking labour

Machines have been replacing human jobs ever since the beginning of the industrial age. In the 18th century, rudimentary machines began automating certain human tasks and further mechanical advancements in the following centuries replaced more and more jobs. Although many jobs have been lost over time, many more new jobs have been created too. In general, both human employment and the number of machines have increased in each phase of the industrial society. On the basis of these historical facts, many assume that the next phase of mechanical technology development – smart machines – will again lead to more and different jobs. However, others expect that smart machines will replace human labour in many areas and dramatically change the nature of work. According to the research firm Gartner, smart machines will enter mainstream adoption by 2021. It expects smart machines to be the most disruptive class of technology over the coming decade.

Smart machines are designed to perform tasks without human intervention, such as in manufacturing and in self-driving cars and self-sailing ships. They merge advanced mechanical technology with digital technologies like computing, artificial intelligence, deep learning, neural networks, voice recognition and natural language processing. Combined with a high data storage capacity that enables smart machines to collect and analyse large volumes of data and algorithms for analysing data and identifying patterns in past and current events, smart machines can calculate what might happen in the future and how best to act. Smart machines are gradually gaining ground as an alternative for human labour. These developments could be 'just another wave in the industrial society' if the economic basis were to remain unchanged. However, one of Adam Smith's growth factors for an industrial society is in jeopardy: labour. As discussed in Chapter 4, Frey and Osborne (2013) concluded that at least 47 percent of the current jobs in America are at risk in the coming decades. And although new jobs will be created, the net outcome of the equation is negative. In another study, Susskind and Susskind (2017) concluded that technology will transform not only low-skilled work that can be automated and robotized, but also the work of skilled professionals. With labour becoming at risk, so is a key pillar of the industrial society's structure: no jobs means no income and no purchasing power for a large number of people.

## Issue 7: Rethinking human life

As already discussed in Chapter 3, three technological developments are now challenging the dominant position of *Homo Sapiens* in society. Firstly, new advances in biotechnology hold out the promise of genetically upgrading humans. Secondly, interfaces between human brains and computers are being developed that may lead to man-machine combinations, also called cyborgs. And thirdly, the combination of artificial intelligence and advanced robotics is leading to human-like beings. These three developments will modify human life itself.

While in history, natural humans have been the single most dominant species on the planet, improved humans, man-robot combinations and new artificial beings are now destined to become part of society, too. For the first time in history, the domination of *Homo Sapiens* (Sapiens 1.0) on the planet is being challenged by genetically modified humans (Sapiens 2.X), upgraded humans (Sapiens 3.X) and artificial human-like beings (Sapiens 4.X). Without interference, these developments may well change societies. It may even lead to societies in which the 'normal humans', Sapiens 1.0, are not dominant anymore but submissive in society, for example because Sapiens 2.X, 3.X and 4.X. are much better equipped to take on many responsibilities, roles and jobs as they are stronger and far more intelligent, possess unlimited memory, do not need to sleep or take vacations and are not afflicted by common human weaknesses such as drinking alcohol. Sapiens 4.X potentially even possesses eternal life, something that humans have been dreaming of since time immemorial.

**Sapiens 2.X: Genetically modified humans**

Biotechnology – the genetic modification of living organisms and their components – is the oldest of the waves of technologies that humans have initiated in their efforts to control nature and improve their lives. The first wave is *horticulture:* the science and art of growing plants (fruits, vegetables, flowers and any other cultivar). It also includes plant conservation, landscape restoration, soil management, landscape and garden design, construction and maintenance, and arboriculture. Historians even suggest that some elements of horticulture (plant conservation and soil management) were already in use by hunters and gatherers and eventually led to the agrarian society.

In the second wave, farmers started improving species of plants and animals by cross-breeding and cross-pollination. In recent years, especially, biotechnology has expanded in sophistication, scope and applicability. With genetic modification, the genes of an organism can be altered, usually independently of the natural reproductive process. Genetic modification can lead to the production of food-bearing plants that are resistant to extreme weather, adverse climates, insect infestations, disease, moulds and fungi. It can also reduce the amount of ploughing in the farming process to save energy and minimise soil erosion.

In the third wave, nanoscience is applied to biotechnology. With nanotechnology, individual atoms and molecules can be manipulated and controlled on the nanometre scale: a billionth of a metre. To give an example, a sheet of newspaper is about 100,000 nanometres thick. Everything on Earth is made up of atoms: the food we eat, the clothes we wear, the buildings and houses we live in and our own bodies. Nanorobots could be programmed to select and destroy bacteria and viruses or single out and kill cancer cells.

Until recently, genetic engineering has focused primarily on agriculture, but humans are now also the subject of research and development. Biotechnology has the potential for human lifespan extension, human cloning and embryonic stem-cell research, while nanotechnology could be used to select and destroy crucial organic cells. The result would be modified humans: Sapiens 2.X.

## Sapiens 3.X: Upgraded humans

In 1960, the visionary psychologist and computer pioneer JCR Licklider wrote[9]: 'In not too many years, human brains and computing machines will be coupled together very tightly, and that the resulting partnership will think as no human brain has ever thought and process data in a way not approached by the information-handling machines we know today.' Licklider helped to launch the information revolution of the past half century, but the full realisation of his vision had to wait a few decades for two technology trends to mature. Currently, interfaces between human brains and computers are being developed that may lead to man-machine combinations (Kaku, 2015). The potential of this combination has been formulated by Bryan Johnson, founder of Kernel, a company that aims to augment human intelligence with AI[10]: 'We have over 80bn neurons in the brain. Our tools currently give us access to an extremely small number of neurons. With prosthetics, we're maybe talking about 100 neurons. We need higher bandwidth interfaces.' Humans are on a path to a more symbiotic union with AI, dubbed 'cyborgs' or – as coined by Elon Musk – 'humans with a neural lace'. Elon Musk intends to be one of them, as he perceives AI as an existential threat to humanity if it goes unchecked[11].

In 2016, Elon Musk[12] founded Neuralink, a neurotechnology company with the aim to develop implantable brain-machine interfaces (BMIs). Neuralink has hired several high-profile neuroscientists from various universities. In 2019, the company announced that it was working on a 'sewing machine-like' device capable of implanting very thin (4 to 6 µm) threads into the brain[13] and anticipated starting experiments with humans in 2020[14]. A neural lace – a digital layer above the cortex – could lead to human enhancement[15]. As of 2020, Neuralink is headquartered in San Francisco's Mission District, sharing the former Pioneer Trunk Factory building with OpenAI, another company co-founded by Musk.

**Sapiens 4.X: Artificial human-like beings**
Human robot Sophia was 'born' on February 14, 2016, and has since been upgraded several times. Sophia is a robot with functional legs and the ability to walk, a 'lifelike skin' with more than 60 facial expressions, scripting software, speech recognition software (from Google's parent company Alphabet), text-to-speech software for chatting and singing and artificial intelligence. Cameras in Sophia's eyes combine with computer algorithms to allow her to see; she can follow faces, sustain eye contact and recognise individuals.

On October 25, 2017, Sophia was granted Saudi Arabian citizenship at the Future Investment Summit in Riyadh, becoming the first robot ever to have a nationality. Sophia's creator, David Hanson of Hanson Robotics, said that Sophia would be a 'social robot' and serve in healthcare, customer service, therapy and education. But Sophia could serve in 'less social' roles too.

## Issue 8: Rethinking natural living

Industrial societies have been – and actually still are and increasingly so – poisoning Mother Earth. Biodiversity, essential to maintaining the cycle of life on our planet, is declining by over 100 species each day as a result of an array of causes such as pollution, poaching, pesticides and over-harvesting (Brannen, 2020). In 150 industrial years, forests dropped from 45% to currently less than 30% of the earth's surface, while nearly 90% of rainforests have been lost for profits in palm oil plantations, wood production and cattle production. Cutting down forests has *reduced consumption* of the greenhouse gas CO2 and also *reduced production* of oxygen. CO2 levels have risen from 260 ppm (parts per million) in 1900 to over 415 ppm in 2020, causing drastic changes in our climate. A major source of greenhouse gases is the livestock sector (Steinfeld et.al, 2006). It is responsible for 18 percent of greenhouse gas emissions and, with regard to man-made emissions, 37 percent of methane, 65 percent of nitrous oxide and 64 percent of ammonia emissions.

Climate change affects oceans, too. Oceans absorb CO2, causing ocean acidification: dissolution of calcium in shellfish and coral reefs and explosive algae blooms that suffocate marine life. The rising temperature causes massive coral reef die-offs, known as 'coral bleaching'. Over the space of fifty years, 25% of all coral reefs worldwide have been turned into ocean dead zones and another 50% is on the brink of collapse. Coral reefs are breeding grounds for many fish populations, so with the collapse of the reefs fish populations are in jeopardy.

Another massive threat to fish populations is overfishing. Each year, an estimated 110 million tonnes of fish are pulled from the ocean, with 25% being caught as 'by-catch' and mostly thrown dead overboard. In 150 industrial years, worldwide fish stocks plummeted by 85% and over half of all fish stocks have fully collapsed. Still, many fisheries are increasing the size of their fleets, subsidised by governments with taxpayers' money. At the current rate there will be no fish left in the oceans by 2045.

Plastic is another major problem for the planet. Plastic materials are impervious to the recycling mechanisms of nature and therefore not biodegradable, and they also contain the 'priority pollutants' (so-called because of their toxicity or persistence in organisms and food webs): heavy metals, pesticides, solvents, flame retarders, UV-protectors, colour stabilisers, aromatic additives and PCBs. We produce 300 million tons of plastic each year, half of it for single-use purposes, and over 8 million tons of plastic is dumped in our oceans and 4 million tons in nature[16]. Only 19 percent is recycled, the rest of it winds up in landfills.

In the ocean, plastics become brittle and break down into microplastics (Smith et.al. 2018) and together with the micro-plastics in washing detergents, soaps, clothes and packaging materials they create 'plastic soup'. Microplastics are too small to be removed from our oceans or filtered out by water treatment plants. The fish we eat, the water we drink and the air we breathe are increasingly polluted with chemicals from plastics. For example, a 2009 study by the Nicolas Pierson Foundation, Bloomberg School of Public Health and the Johns Hopkins University Center for a Livable Future advised pregnant women to refrain from consuming fish as it can contain heavy metals like mercury and cadmium.

Another harmful residue comes from widely used pesticides in agriculture. Many people consume weedkiller residues in food, such as children's breakfast cereals, and this can cause cancer. Gut bacteria play a vital role in maintaining good health, not only in humans but also in other organisms, like honey bees. Pesticides harm some of the key beneficial bacteria in bees' guts, affecting bee health and their effectiveness as pollinators[17] and causing increased mortality in honey bee colonies. The global decline in honey bees is one of the major causes of habitat loss.

In short, industrial societies are poisoning human life.

***Notes***

1 Lorenz, Edward N. 'Deterministic Nonperiodic Flow', Journal of the Atmospheric Sciences, March 1963, 20 (2): 130–141.

2 In Amsterdam there is even a 'Party Against Scooters'.

3 World Economic Forum is a UN partner.

4 The Canadian Press, 'Ottawa sued over Quebec fracking ban: company's suit based on NAFTA provisions', ***CBC News***, Nov 23, 2012.

5 Foreign Affairs Trade and Development, Government of Canada, 'Eli Lilly and Company v. Government of Canada', January 20, 2017.

6 United Nations Conference on Trade And Development (UNCTAD), '***Recent Developments in Investor-State Dispute Settlement (ISDS): Updated for the Multilateral Dialogue on Investment***', 28-29 May 2013.

7 CETA, pages 158–161.

8 Corporate Europe Observatory, 'ECJ confirms legality of unfair corporate tribunals in EU trade deals', 30 April 2019.

9 Licklider, 'Man-Computer Symbiosis', ***Transactions on Human Factors in Electronics***, volume HFE-1, pp. 4–11, March 1960

10 Nick Statt, Kernel is trying to hack the human brain – but neuroscience has a long way to go', ***The Verge***, Feb 22, 2017.

11 Isobel Asher Hamilton, 'Elon Musk believes AI could turn humans into an endangered species like the mountain gorilla', ***Business Insider***, 26 November 2018

12 Together with Ben Rapoport, Dongjin Seo, Max Hodak, Paul Merolla, Philip Sabes, Tim Gardner, Tim Hanson, and Vanessa Tolosa

13 Elizabeth Lopatto, 'Elon Musk unveils Neuralink's plans for brain-reading 'threads' and a robot to insert them', ***The Verge***. 16 July 2019.

14 John Markoff, 'Elon Musk's Company Takes Baby Steps to Wiring Brains to the Internet', ***The New York Times***. July 16, 2019).

15 Annalee Newitz, 'Elon Musk is setting up a company that will link brains and computers', ***Ars Technica***. March 27, 2017.

16 Pabortsava, Katsiaryna & Richard S. Lampitt (2020).

17 Erick V. S. Motta, Kasie Raymann, and Nancy A. Moran, 'Glyphosate perturbs the gut microbiota of honey bees', ***Proceedings of the National Academy of Sciences***, September 24, 2018.

# THE ELITE RESET SOCIETY

# 6

At the peak of the corona crisis in 2020, Klaus Schwab, founder and Executive Chairman of the World Economic Forum, and Thierry Malleret, founder of the Monthly Barometer, published the book *COVID-19: The Great Reset*[1], claiming to provide 'a guide for anyone who wants to understand how COVID-19 disrupted our social and economic systems, and what changes will be needed to create a more inclusive, resilient and sustainable world going forward.' With the term '*Great Reset*' the authors expressed their expectation regarding the near future.

The Great War between 1914 and 1918, with 22 million deaths and millions more due to the 1918 pandemic, was meant to be 'the war to end all wars', yet a little over twenty years later came the outbreak of the Second World War and the Holocaust. The Great Depression, which started on the infamous Black Tuesday in 1929, caused a huge and devastating global economic meltdown. Unemployment rates ranged between 22 and 33 percent in many countries and global gross domestic product (GDP) fell by 15 percent. The Great Recession in 2007 took hold of much of society following the bursting of the US housing bubble, the subprime mortgage and derivatives fiasco and the resulting bailouts, all of which led to a substantial drop in GDP in many countries and increased levels of unemployment. And the date March 11, 2020, when coronavirus was declared 'a pandemic' by the WHO, has now been declared 'The Great Reset' by Klaus Schwab and Thierry Malleret. According to the International Labour Organisation (ILO) 'some 1.6 billion people employed in the informal economy – or nearly half the global workforce – could see their livelihoods destroyed due to the continued decline in working hours brought on by lockdowns to curb the spread of COVID-19.' In addition, the IMF has warned of 'the worst financial crisis since the Great Depression' and the UN Labour Agency expects 'nearly half of global workforce at risk as job losses increase due to COVID-19'[2].

The way the World Economic Forum has reacted to the Covid-19 'pandemic' illustrates how it envisions a new world order and how it views the 'Great Reset'. As the pandemic is a global health issue, the WEF aligned itself closely with the WHO in issuing the mission statement: 'Better health for everyone, everywhere. We are building a better, healthier future for people all over the world'. The WHO is a multinational NGO with 150 offices on six continents, cooperating with 194 member states and many multinational enterprises (corporate-states), global citizens and charities in the 'health domain'. The interests of these stakeholders specified 'better health for everyone' and defined the best route to globally curbing the 'pandemic'. This is what founder and Executive Chairman of the World Economic Forum Klaus Schwaab refers to as 'stakeholder capitalism'[3].

## Stakeholder capitalism?

The term 'stakeholder capitalism' was first introduced by Adolf A. Berle and Gardiner C. Means in their book *The Modern Corporation and Private Property* (1932). The authors argued that company leaders should balance the claims of different stakeholders, taking into account public policy. However, since the publication of Milton Friedman's *New York Times Magazine* article 'The Social Responsibility of Business is to Increase its Profits' in 1970, the twentieth century and the beginning of the twenty-first century have been dominated by 'shareholder capitalism'.

Schwaab's re-introduction of the term 'stakeholder capitalism' suggests that he embraces Berle and Means' original perspective that shareholder value should be balanced with public values. Yet, Schwaab also holds the divergent thought that only *some* stakeholders are involved: corporate-states, NGOs, global citizens and global charities. This situation has been described by Steve Denning[4] as follows: 'Firms can go on privately shovelling money to their shareholders and executives, while maintaining a public front of exquisite social sensitivity and exemplary altruism.'

In order to achieve their missions and visions, corporate-states, NGOs, global charities and global citizens attempt to influence social debates, citizens and political choices. In doing so, they make use of a menu of 'advocacy tactics'[5]: information politics, symbolic politics, leverage politics and accountability politics. The most influential devices are information politics (providing technical information) and leverage politics (shaming, lobbying and cooperating with other organisations) and they are most effective when applied in a 'society-above-society structure'[6] in which the state, in cooperation with an elite, exercises significant control over society – the preferred situation of the 'global stakeholder capitalists'. Their influence is least effective in a 'liberal structure' where citizens and societal groups are central in developing policy, with a limited role for the elite – a situation they would prefer to avoid.

The Elite Reset Society aims to resolve the eight societal issues in the previous chapter as follows:

## Issue 1 (Rethinking the nation-state concept): Divide and rule

Many corporate-states are now more powerful than nation-states, and in order to become even more powerful in the years ahead the new elite may use one of the oldest strategies of the military, foreign policy and politics: 'divide and rule' (in Latin: divide et impera). Military leaders who employed this strategy include Philip II of Macedonia, the Roman ruler Julius Caesar and the French emperor Napoleon. The strategy has been formulated in many documents, such as Book VI of *The Art of War* by Niccolò Machiavelli[7]: *'A Captain should endeavour with every art to divide the forces of the enemy'*[8].

Of crucial importance to the elite is their aim to divide and rule the largest states, such as the United States, Russia, China and India. These countries form a threat, as they are large enough to distance themselves from the 'new global reality' and also as they may become a 'Big Brother' sheltering smaller countries against the interests of corporate-states and their allies. Large states could be economically weakened by moving human labour, investments and production facilities (such as data centres) abroad and avoiding taxes. Nation-states could also be weakened by increasing the state's financial dependence on global financial companies, their shareholders and other financial players.

In the *Elite Reset Society*, supra-state unions, such as the European Union, must be manipulated, frustrated and preferably also weakened. For example, the departure of Great Britain from the European Union is a blessing for corporate-states and a 'best case' to derive learnings that can be applied elsewhere. A next step could be to stimulate other countries to leave the European Union, such as a 'Nexit' (exit of the Netherlands). While supranational unions remain in existence, they could be controlled by corporate-states' representatives that advocate their interests. Policy papers could be influenced and alternative perspectives censured.[9]

However, most threatening are global public initiatives aimed at strengthening nation-states or 'virtual citizen communities'. States or groups of civilians that develop alternative and competing global public and commercial systems must be blocked or frustrated. The classic 'divide and rule' strategy consists of several techniques to weaken counterforces of united citizens: polarisation between social groups, preventing alliances between social groups, aiding and promoting those who are willing to cooperate, fostering distrust and enmity between social groups and encouraging meaningless expenditures that reduce the strength of counterforces.

## Issue 2 (Rethinking the governance of societies): Societal control

Capital has become the strongest societal factor and over time it will be the only factor. Capital will be in power and many of the 'capital holders' will mould the economy and society to serve their interests. The most straightforward route to direct control of society is to take over government and form an oligarchy with a 'Country CEO' as president, appointed by the capital holders. However, in a democracy this would be risky, as it may mobilise societal counterforces with an uncertain outcome. The second best option is to achieve indirect control by influencing democratic processes but leaving the system intact. From a distance, society then remains unchanged as an 'industrial society' and continues to be called an industrial society ('the fourth industrial revolution') but it will be indirectly controlled. Indirect control can be realised through four streams of influence:

Firstly, capital holders can strengthen their influence on political positions at all political levels. They will support political candidates that promise to serve the interests of the capital holders and political decisions will be prepared and implemented in their interest, backed by the enforcement of an authority such as the police or the army.

Secondly, another crucial factor can be control over the provision of information to citizens. Capital owners will need to own or control the media and the messages they send, including social media like Facebook and LinkedIn. Non-compliant information will be censored and the credibility and reputation of the authors of such information will be attacked and undermined by trolls and fake profiles and their profiles will be removed. Fake profiles will be used to send fake messages that are intentionally misconstrued.

Thirdly, societal counterforces and dissidents need to be contained as soon as possible and at all cost, as this is the main threat to indirect control over society. As a rule of thumb, when more than 25 percent of citizens form a concerted countermovement, societal control is at stake. An effective means of preventing and curbing counterforces is to create the fear of an enemy, stimulate polarisation among societal groups and isolate or compromise dissidents.

Fourthly, the economic agenda has to serve the interests of capital holders. As the capital holders have a stake in large companies, all crucial basic human needs have to be economically controlled and exploited, including food, energy, health, media and social platform communication, transportation and education. Local and private initiatives, such as the decentralised production of energy and food and decentralised bartering, should be discouraged.

## Issue 3 (Rethinking world governance): World government

Global companies will need to cooperate with a number of non-governmental organisations. Some NGOs have a strong position in their professional domain and the power to develop global rules and standards, such as the World Health Organisation (WHO), World Economic Forum (WEF) and International Energy Agency (IEA), while other NGOs are related to charities run by global citizens with specific objectives, such as the Bill and Melinda Gates Foundation and the Rockefeller Foundation.

As the number of players per domain is limited and world governance is not based on democratic processes, mutual alignment and decision-making are relatively orderly. A 'World Government' for commercially attractive domains, such as health, is possible. The main aim of a (formal or informal) World Government is to influence decision-making in nation-states, as many NGOs for human rights, women's rights and environmental protection have experienced. However, in these domains the revenue model is based on voluntary donations and so their impact is limited. In other domains, such as health care, alignment between global companies is extremely fruitful. NGOs' global power influences choices in nation-states, while maintaining access to abundant financial resources and an extremely profitable business case.

## Issue 4 (Rethinking industrial capitalism): Oligarchical capitalism

Over one hundred years ago, in 1915, Robert Michaels wrote[10]: 'All complex organisations, regardless of how democratic they are when started, eventually develop into oligarchies. Democratic attempts (...) are prone to fail, since with power comes the ability to reward loyalty, the ability to control information, and the ability to control what procedures the organisation follows when making decisions.' Michaels also stated that the democratic objective of preventing an elite from ruling is impossible in the long run and that oligarchy is inevitable. By controlling access to information, the elite can centralise power, often with little accountability. They can do so because of the apathy, indifference and non-participation of the majority of people. This is what Piketty (2014) has called 'patrimonial capitalism', in which much of the economy is dominated by inherited wealth. Intelligence data could then be the future version of landownership in the feudal society, with data being the most important resource of value creation, intelligence the main control mechanism and smart robots the defending soldiers.

Two versions of oligarchy have existed previously in history. The first is a society with a rich elite plus everyone else, as in the feudal society (explained in chapter 2). In that case, as Plato stated more than 2,300 years ago, 'there will be a society of the rich and a society of the poor, always plotting against one another.' But this version existed before the industrial wave and when the elite had no economic driver to develop some wealth for the remaining citizens.

The second version of oligarchy consists of three societal groups: an elite, a middle class and the poor (the have-alls, the have-somethings and the have-nothings). As there is currently a well-developed middle class as a result of the industrial age, some middle class will remain in the future. In addition, the elite has a compelling economic argument to maintain a middle class. There must be sufficient market demand for the products and services of their companies to keep the economic engine running and increase their wealth and that of their shareholders. At the same time, the elite can use their power to increase their share of the created economic value.

In this version, the middle class will be maintained and the poor will suffer. Inequality between the elite and the middle class will be 'just-right' as Freeman (2015) wrote, in order not to mobilise strong counterforces. The middle class will be the servants and submissive to the elite; any action that might undermine their interests will be suppressed ruthlessly. China's Citizen Score ('Social Credit Score') system, with its digital technologies like Big Data and Artificial Intelligence and 900 million surveillance cameras in the streets, is a good example. Corporate-states are well capable of monitoring which citizens are potentially dangerous to their possessions and interests and which citizens may be planning to take action.

## Issue 5 (Rethinking income distribution): Elite haves

Oligarchical capitalism is the modern version of landownership in the feudal society, with data being the most important resource of value creation, intelligence the main control mechanism and smart robots the defending soldiers. This would lead to a three-class, unequal society with have-alls, have-somethings and have-nots. The have-alls will have access to the Sapiens 2.X modifications and the Sapiens 3.X upgrades.

In the West, the have-alls will consist of families and companies that gain control over intelligent data. Potential candidates are families that have collected large financial resources in past societal waves, such as Rothschild (banking), Rockefeller (oil), Morgan (banking), Du Pont (chemicals) and Bush (banking) (Bernish, 2016), as well as high-tech companies like Microsoft, Apple, Google, Amazon and Tesla. In autocratic countries such as Russia, South Korea, Turkey and, particularly, China, country leaders will be the have-alls, alongside company leaders like Jack Ma (originally Ma Yun, Alibaba). The 'haves' – the industrial aristocracy – are likely to possess the means to control the relevant technology companies through ownership, as well as the power to control intelligent data and protect themselves from intruders. They would then have exclusive access to the technologies that would allow them to become man-machine combinations and upgrade themselves with biotechnology. Human-like robots (Sapiens 4.X) would then be at their disposal as a cheap and reliable alternative for Sapiens 1.0.

The have-somethings will consist of the have-alls' retinues, i.e. the professional entourage serving the have-alls. All others will belong to the have-nots, who will not be connected to the global society of intelligent data. The have-somethings will mainly be consumers with access to the produce of the global elite. Without their money there would be a negative trend in consumer spending with all kinds of effects that are in nobody's interest, such as an economic recession and social anxiety. In addition, have-somethings will be locally active with their friends and families, thereby maintaining local economies.

## Issue 6 (Rethinking labour): Resource optimisation

Humans will be replaced by technologies such as robots and smart machines. The combination of advanced machines and digital technologies, in particular, will increasingly be more productive than humans in many business activities. However, when humans are 'cheaper' they may still be employed. In some business activities, humans will still be needed, especially in business domains that require human interaction, such as hairdressers and bars. As a value creating resource, humans have many weaknesses. For example, they become ill, need sleep and a private life, want to take vacations, organise in unions to get better pay and working conditions and need permanent education. Alternative production means, such as human-like robots and smart machines, require less attention and managerial time and are therefore more competitive as resources than 'human resources'.

## Issue 7 (Rethinking human life): Elite upgrade

Humans can be upgraded with new biotechnology developments such as the CRISPR-Cas-9 technology, with which human DNA can be manipulated. As a result there will be modified humans: Sapiens 2.X. Humans can also be upgraded by implanting brain-machine interfaces (BMIs), leading to what Elon Musk calls 'humans with a neural lace', also called cyborgs. These upgraded humans 3.X may have an IQ of 300 or higher. The difference compared with the intelligence of the current Sapiens 1.0 is huge – comparable to the IQ difference between humans and chimpanzees. And human-like robots with artificial intelligence, such as Sophia, will lead to artificial human beings (4.X) that potentially possess eternal life.

With the arrival of Sapiens 2.X, 3.X and 4.X, *Homo Sapiens* will no longer be the superior species on earth. The elite will have the power and money to upgrade themselves before others do. In that case, the upgraded elite will be superior to the rest of humanity. The difference between them and other humans on the planet will be too large to be vulnerable to attacks on their position. With a combination of power, billions of dollars, access to technology and genetical and IQ upgrades, a cyborg elite will be able to rule the world. Sapiens 4.X will become the servants and soldiers protecting them. Their position will then be secure for as long as Mother Earth allows.

## Issue 8 (Rethinking natural living): Coalition of the winning

Restoring nature and the climate needs globally directed, fundamental and fast interventions from corporate-states, NGOs, global citizens and charitable organisations. The problems of nature and climate are just too large for national governments and small businesses. For example, 'The Future Of Nature' report by the World Economic Forum (2020) estimates that 'building a nature-positive economy could represent more than $10 trillion per year by

2030 - in terms of new economic opportunities as well as avoided economic costs.' The massive challenge can then be seen as an opportunity: 'In the short term, deploying around $250 billion of stimulus funding could generate up to 37 million nature-positive jobs in a highly cost-effective manner. Resetting the environment should not be seen as a cost, but rather an investment that will generate economic activity and employment opportunities.'

Given that the problems with nature and the climate are urgent and building a 'nature-positive' economy also represents an opportunity, a winning coalition of global players is a superior road forward when compared with waiting for cooperative initiatives between countries. These initiatives are ineffective and take too much time, and will probably not lead to solutions. Governments should be given clear guidelines on how to proceed, directed by the winning coalition of global players. The harsh economic consequences of the 'corona pandemic' provide a favourable context for the societal reforms required to rescue nature and the climate, and therefore Planet Earth.

The 17 Sustainable Development Goals (SDGs)[11] of the United Nations may well serve as the strategic agenda for the coalition of the winning. The SDGs, set out in 2015 by the United Nations General Assembly and intended to be achieved by the year 2030, are part of a UN Resolution called the '2030 Agenda'[12]. On June 2017, the Rockefeller Foundation hosted a workshop that concluded that 'while there is a moral imperative to achieve the SDGs, failure is inevitable if there aren't drastic changes to how we go about financing large scale change.' Drastic changes need the support, financing and leadership of the elite.

***Notes***

[1] It is actually quite remarkable that this 280-page book was published at the peak of the Covid-19 outbreak, on 9 July 2020, including translations in German, French, Spanish, Japanese and Mandarin Chinese.

[2] UN News, 28 April 2020.

[3] Schwaab, ***The Global Reset: The Case for Stakeholder Capitalism***, John Wiley & Sons Inc, 30 December 2020.

[4] Steve Denning, Why Stakeholder Capitalism Will Fail, ***Forbes***, January 5, 2020.

[5] Keck, Margaret E. & Kathryn Sikkink, 'Transnational Advocacy Networks in International and Regional Politics', International Social Science Journal, 1999, 51 (159): 89-101.

[6] Checkel, Jeffrey T., 'International Norms and Domestic Politics: Bridging the Rationalist-Constructivist Divide', European Journal of International Relations, 1997, 3(4), 473-495.

[7] Niccolò Machiavelli, ***The Art of War*** (L'arte della guerra), 1521.

[8] Many other documents refer to the strategy of divide and rule, including Sun Tzu in '***The Art of War***' (5th Century BC), Edward Coke (in Chapter I of the Fourth Part of the '***Institutes of the Lawes of England***', Sir Francis Bacon in a letter to James I of 15 February 1615, James Madison in a letter of 24 October 1787 to Thomas Jefferson, Immanuel Kant in '***Perpetual Peace: A Philosophical Sketch***' (1795), and Karl von Clausewitz in '***On War***' (1832).

[9] See for an example: 'Tackling COVID-19 disinformation - Getting the facts right' by the High Representative of the Union for Foreign Affairs of the European Commission, Brussels, 10 June 2020.

[10] Robert Michaels, 'Political Parties: A Sociological Study of the Oligarchical Tendencies of Modern Democracy', 1915, p. 241. Translation: Eden and Cedar Paul, Kitchener, Ontario: Batoche Books, 2001.

[11] The 17 SDGs are: (1) No Poverty, (2) Zero Hunger, (3) Good Health and Well-being, (4) Quality Education, (5) Gender Equality, (6) Clean Water and Sanitation, (7) Affordable and Clean Energy, (8) Decent Work and Economic Growth, (9) Industry, Innovation and Infrastructure, (10) Reducing Inequality, (11) Sustainable Cities and Communities, (12) Responsible Consumption and Production, (13) Climate Action, (14) Life Below Water, (15) Life On Land, (16) Peace, Justice, and Strong Institutions, (17) Partnerships for the Goals.

[12] United Nations Resolution adopted by the General Assembly on 25 September 2015, Transforming our world: the 2030 Agenda for Sustainable Development; United Nations, Resolution adopted by the General Assembly on 6 July 2017, Work of the Statistical Commission pertaining to the 2030 Agenda for Sustainable Development.

# THE GLOCAL CITIZENS SOCIETY

# 7

The *Elite Reset Society* is the future scenario that extrapolates current developments as described in previous chapters. Yet history has shown that such a scenario has never become the new end state. Although ruling powers have always aimed to keep their privileged position, societies have changed because citizens started to fight for a better future. Arguably the most distinct example in the West has been the case of The Netherlands in the 16th century.

**Declaration of independence**

On 26 July 1581, the Dutch people freed themselves from Spanish rule with the 'Placard of Abjuration'[1], a declaration of independence. It was the first time in European history that a people successfully renounced a sovereign because of his failure to be a king and formed an independent republic[2]. The States General of the United Provinces of the Low Countries, as the Netherlands was then (and occasionally still is) called, wrote (bold italics added):

> 'As it is apparent to all that a prince is constituted by God to be ruler of a people, to defend them from oppression and violence as the shepherd his sheep; and whereas God did not create the people slaves to their prince, to obey his commands, whether right or wrong, but rather the prince for the sake of the subjects (without which he could be no prince), to govern them according to equity, to love and support them as a father his children or a shepherd his flock, and even at the hazard of life to defend and preserve them. And ***when he does not behave thus, but, on the contrary, oppresses them, seeking opportunities to infringe their ancient customs and privileges, exacting from them slavish compliance, then he is no longer a prince, but a tyrant, and the subjects are to consider him in no other view.*** And particularly when this is done deliberately, unauthorized by the states, they may not only disallow his authority, but legally proceed to the choice of another prince for their defense. This is the only method left for subjects whose humble petitions and remonstrances could never soften their prince or dissuade him from his tyrannical proceedings; and this is what the law of nature dictates for the defense of liberty, which we ought to transmit to posterity, even at the hazard of our lives.'

The 'Placard of Abjuration' was an unprecedented, brave and revolutionary document, yet it was received with skepsis by the noblemen (as already noted in Chapter 2) who asked: 'How could a motley collection of tradesmen, salt dealers, fishermen, and tallow chandlers hope to govern themselves without royal or even noble guidance?' The Placard has inspired many others in Europe and abroad, such as the United States, which declared itself free from the United Kingdom with the 'Declaration of Independence'.

Current citizen initiatives are also being met with skepsis by powerful organisations and individuals, such as the citizens movement known as the 'Commons[3]'. The term 'Commons' has been defined by Estrom (1990) as 'a social practice of governing a resource not by state or market but by a community of users that self-governs the resource through institutions that it creates.' Commons can be understood as resources that are managed by groups of people (communities, user groups) for individual and collective benefit (Basu, Jongerden and Ruivenkamp, 2017) and not by owners or government (Bollier, David and Silke Helfrich, 2012).

Citizens' movements can inspire people to reinvent society. Based on the issues addressed in Chapter 5, the future society could be as follows:

## Issue 1 (Rethinking the nation-state concept): Glocal citizen communities

Demarcation of land started when warlords claimed land and became aristocratic landlords. Over time, landowners' properties came to mark the territorial borders of nation-states. Since then, many historical events, such as wars and other conflicts, have served to shift borders numerous times. The result is that the current territorial borders of nation-states are the coincidental result of past events. They are literally shadows of the past.

Over time, the horizon of citizens broadened from regional to global. Whereas in the Agricultural Age people had to travel by foot, by horse or by coach and so with very limited reach, today people can fly by airplane to the other side of the planet within 24 hours. And with the rise of the Internet and social platforms, people can now connect digitally with family, friends and other social partners anywhere in the world. Digitally, people have become global citizens with membership of communities worldwide, while physically living and working in one region. Their digital identity is based on personal choices and preferences, while their physical identity relates to where they were born and raised and to the place where they live and work. People have become global citizens and they also want to be able to exercise influence in their personal domain, which is usually a combination of local and global. They are *glocal* citizens.

The important issues for citizens are increasingly at the local level – their direct living and working environment – and on the global scale – personal interests and worries such as climate change. At the local level, citizens have some influence, yet this is limited to choosing leaders with views on what the issues are and how to deal with them. From there, leaders decide top-down on regional topics. On the global scale, citizens have no influence at all: global organisations such as the UN and NGOs are not democracies and decisions are made by undemocratically appointed leaders with certain ideas and financial interests, and in undemocratic networks of public and private organisations and other stakeholders.

If we were able to design societies from scratch today, with no shadows of the past, nation-states would probably not be invented. We would build a digital platform to connect all people and then citizens would form or join communities with people who share the same interests. Some of these communities would consist of people at the local level discussing and deciding on local issues, while other communities would be regional and global: topical and personal.

Public space should then consist of a public digital platform, connecting citizens all over the globe who personalise their digital domains. Indeed, such digital platforms exist already, with dominant players like (the corporate-states) Facebook and LinkedIn. However, these (often) oligopolistic platforms are in the hands of shareholders and make choices in the interests of those shareholders, with company leaders striving to maximise shareholder value. To achieve this objective, everything that is legally permitted is implemented, including setting or changing algorithms and censuring on the basis of the company's interests as formulated in its 'terms and conditions'. Company leadership decides top-down on the basis of commercial and private – not public – values.

The future digital social platforms should therefore be owned by communities of citizens, with terms and conditions that are democratically decided by citizens to serve public interests. Application of the terms and conditions could be achieved with the help of deep learning (AI) technology, so that activities are implemented immediately and flawlessly.

## Issue 2 (Rethinking the governance of societies): Swarm intelligence decisions

Another shadow of the past manifests itself in the way in which decisions are made. Fighting for and protecting the land were military activities, with warlords and army leaders making decisions and telling soldiers what to do. Human communities and countries were led top-down. Also, in democracies, citizens vote for their leaders based on what these leaders promise they will do.

In times without direct digital connections, this was the only way to lead a country or a city.

However, a public digital social platform that connects citizens all over the world can be applied for governance purposes as well by making use of what is known as the 'wisdom of the crowd'[4]. Decision-making by a large group of citizens captures the wisdom of the crowd, which exceeds the wisdom of each individual, including that of experts. This phenomenon was ignored for almost a century after it was first described in 1907 by statistician Francis Galton. In 1906, Galton organised a contest with 800 people at a country fair in Plymouth to estimate the weight of a slaughtered ox. He observed that the median guess, 1207 pounds, was accurate to within 1% of the true weight of 1198 pounds (Galton, 1907) – much more accurate than each individual guess within the group of 800 people.

The explanation for the 'wisdom of the crowd' phenomenon lies in the idiosyncratic noise associated with each individual judgment. Taking the average over a large number of responses cancels out the effect of this noise (Yi et.al, 2012). The conditions required for capturing the wisdom of the crowd include sufficient diversity in the group (with a large diversity the error of the crowd is small; Page, 2007) and the absence of social influencing (Lorenz et. Al, 2011). The popularity of the 'wisdom of the crowd' phenomenon has increased in the digital age thanks to social information sites such as Quora, Stack Exchange, Wikipedia and other web resources that rely on collective human knowledge (Baase, 2017).

In nature, the 'wisdom of the crowd' phenomenon is known as 'swarm intelligence'. Interaction between thousands of individual animals within a swarm of birds, fish or bees leads to intelligent swarm behaviour (Bleijenberg, 2020). Swarm intelligence emerges from the collective behaviour of decentralised, self-organising animals. In a swarm there is no centralised top-down control structure dictating how individual members should behave. They follow very simple rules, such as 'eat, don't be eaten and reproduce'. Individual swarm members are not aware of the swarm intelligence at the higher level.

Large groups of citizens can also capture swarm intelligence when public digital social platforms are used with the aim of making the right decisions. Swarm decisions can not only be made on the individual people representing these citizens, but also – and even especially – on complex topics. 'Digital citizens' voting on complex topics on digital social platforms can capture swarm intelligence and, using deep learning software, intelligent conclusions can then be derived. Decision-making becomes bottom-up and the individual leaders who are assigned a specific role by citizens implement the decisions.

## Issue 3 (Rethinking world governance): Honourable humans

The world's main governing organisation is the United Nations (UN), an intergovernmental organisation with the objective of 'maintaining international peace and security, protecting human rights, delivering humanitarian aid, promoting sustainable development, and upholding international law.' The organisation is financed by voluntary contributions from its member states. The UN has 193 member states and is headquartered in New York City, with other main offices in Geneva, Nairobi, Vienna and The Hague. Some non-governmental organisations (NGOs) have consultative status with the Economic and Social Council (ECOSOC) and specialised agencies, such as the World Bank Group, the World Health Organisation, the World Food Programme, UNESCO and UNICEF, participate in the UN's work.

The current status of the UN is mixed: it is praised for being an important vehicle for peace and human development and criticised for being ineffective, biased and corrupt. The UN receives feedback on its activities from the member states but it has no other democratic feedback system in place. Given that decision-making at the United Nations is currently not based on democratic processes and its members are not democratically appointed, the UN cannot be considered a democracy. Citizens are not involved, which leaves the organisation open to influence by corporate-states, NGOs, global citizens and global charities. They are able to influence choices at the United Nations thanks to their abundant financial resources. In addition, over 2,000 NGOs are officially accredited by the UN and are automatically granted the right to participate in UN-sponsored conferences, thereby influencing decision-making at the UN. Although many NGOs do great work, they lack representativeness and many are accused of being undemocratic and accountable only to those who provide them with funding.

Members of the UN need to be outstanding, honourable citizens with a track record of ethical behaviour, proven by deep learning technology and chosen by means of a democratic process. An example of how members of the UN could be appointed is the way in which citizenship in the Netherlands of the 17th century was achieved. The most important condition for citizenship at that time was *honourable public behaviour*, which gave the citizen the right to become a member of communities. In the same vein, only honourable citizens should be allowed to become a member of the United Nations, with membership being subject to a combination of rights (solidarity) and duties (loyalty). Public digital social platforms with deep learning software could be used for the bottom-up election of honourable citizens and for decision-making on complex topics.

## Issue 4 (Rethinking industrial capitalism): Community currencies

Ever since the early days in mankind's history, there has been a means of measuring relative value when bartering goods and services. This relative value has long been expressed in terms of the weight of precious metals, such as gold, silver and bronze. In the industrial society, however, a monetary system was developed on the basis of trust in central banks and the government. However, this instrument of the capitalist system gradually became oppressive for citizens. Money became more a tool for gaining power and less a means of exchanging value.

An alternative could be *community currencies*, based on the experiences of local currencies that have been around already for over 150 years. Local currencies are usually introduced in response to economic depressions or money scarcity. One of the most successful local currencies was the Swiss WIR, introduced during the Great Depression of 1934. The WIR inspired many other local currencies, such as the Sardex[5] on Sardinia, Italy, in 2009. Using blockchain technology, alternative decentralised value exchanges for public and private goods could replace current monetary systems, not only for local communities but also for global communities.

Local and community currencies aim to encourage paying for or exchanging local or community services. Currently, around 300 local and community currencies are listed in the Complementary Currency Resource Center worldwide database[6]. For example, the Fureai kippu system in Japan issues credits in exchange for assistance to senior citizens, with the result that construction work can be exchanged for community services such as elderly care. Some community currencies even have a global reach, such as Tencent's QQ coins in China, a digital currency for virtual products and services like ringtones and on-line video game time.

Local and community currencies have a catalytic effect on local economies and communities, especially when there is a lack of purchasing power and high unemployment. These community currencies stimulate economic activities between glocal citizens who offer their services to neighbours, friends and all kinds of global community members. Well-developed community currency systems would underpin and strengthen the building of civil societies.

## Issue 5 (Rethinking income distribution): Equal just-right

The primary objective of human societies is ensuring the well-being of as many of its citizens as possible. One key factor that influences human well-being is the level of inequality. In their 2009 book *The Spirit Level*, Wilkinson and Pickett[7] argue that there are 'pernicious effects of inequality on societies: eroding trust, increasing anxiety and illness, and encouraging excessive consumption.' They claim that 'in more unequal countries, whether rich or poor', eleven different health and social problems are significantly more severe: physical health, mental health, drug abuse, education, imprisonment, obesity, social mobility, trust and community life, violence, teenage pregnancies and child well-being. Other studies have also found evidence of a relationship between inequality and health and social problems (MacInnes et al., 2015).

The relationship between inequality and welfare – the economy – has been debated by many economists[8], as in Simon Kuznets' contribution to the annual meeting of the American Economic Association in 1954[9]. Richard Freeman's 2011 hypothesis that 'too much inequality has a negative impact on the economy' has received much support[10].

The overall conclusion is that inequality leads to health and social problems (well-being) and that too much inequality has a negative impact on the economy (welfare). A healthy society for all citizens should therefore place a cap on the maximum share of national income of the country's top 10% richest people, a measure that could even be enshrined in law. For example, the 'just-right inequality' principle – not too little, not too much – could be fixed at a maximum of 40 percent for the 10% richest people, with a middle class consisting of a minimum of 40 percent of the total population and not earning more than 10 times the income of the 'lower class'.

## Issue 6 (Rethinking labour): Producing consumers

As discussed in Chapter 4, the economic engine of the industrial economy has been employment but the future economy will not be based on paid labour, as full employment for citizens will not be an achievable goal in the near future. There is a need for a different economic system. In this system, the role of government needs to change as well. The role of government in the industrial economy has been heavily debated by economists[11] in relation to a variety of capitalist models, such as 'moral capitalism', 'conscious capitalism', 'stakeholder capitalism', 'responsible capitalism' and 'progressive capitalism'. However, within capitalist models, governments have a limited number of effective instruments, with taxation being the main instrument. When Marxist models are taken out of the equation, it means that a new economic model needs to be developed.

The most promising new economic model is one based on the decentralised production of common human necessities such as food and energy. Technologies such as robotics and 3D printing will enable the decentralised and local production of food (vegetables and fruit) and energy. In this decentralised economic model, blockchain technology provides the infrastructure and enables citizens to sell and trade products on the basis of new digital local and community currencies. Using this blockchain network, citizens can also barter services such as helping the elderly and disabled people. Consumers become producers.

The decentralised economic model will not replace the industrial model entirely. It will complement the remaining paid labour, as consumers will not be able to produce large items such as cars and ships in their backyards. Splitting working hours on the basis of decentralised production and part-time jobs will give citizens a *basic income* from both community work and paid labour (Keen, 2018)[12].

This *basic income* model differs from most existing initiatives, as it is based on building a decentralised local economy and not on recirculating taxpayers' money with the government at the head of the system. Recirculating taxpayers' money could in many cases be more efficient – government overhead costs are often significant when calculating and paying unemployment and social moneys – but it cannot facilitate the necessary system change. The new basic income model should boost citizens' well-being.

## Issue 7 (Rethinking human life): Human rights

As already mentioned in Chapter 3, three technological developments are posing a challenge to the human population on Earth: genetically modified humans (Sapiens 2.X), upgraded humans (Sapiens 3.X) and artificial human-like beings (Sapiens 4.X).

Genetic modifications (Sapiens 2.X) should be legally restricted to repairing DNA genomes, as in the case of the HIV-infected father of the Chinese twins Lulu and Nana. Children can be protected from genetic diseases like Alzheimer's and HIV. The list would have to be approved by the UN's 'Honourable Swarm'.

The same rules should apply to upgrading humans with technology such as artificial intelligence, memory aids and robotics (Sapiens 3.X). Humans with deficiencies like a low IQ (below 80 points), damaged memory capacity and physical handicaps (such as lost arms or legs) should be helped. Human upgrades (cyborgs) without the reasons described above should be forbidden by law.

Artificial human-like beings (Sapiens 4.X) such as Sophia can easily be abused by a powerful elite and should follow, at the very least, Asimov's 'Three Laws of Robotics' (Asimov, 1950, 1964):

**First Law**: A robot may not injure a human being or, through inaction, allow a human being to come to harm.

**Second Law**: A robot must obey the orders given it by human beings except where such orders would conflict with the First Law.

**Third Law**: A robot must protect its own existence as long as such protection does not conflict with the First or Second Law.

Artificial human-like beings should be given a legal basis with a transhuman code.

## Issue 8 (Rethinking natural living): Natural harmony

Humans must return to living in harmony with nature in order to save the biosphere, biodiversity and natural resources (Brennan, 2020). The current imbalance between nature and humanity may even increase, as the human population is expected to expand further. '*There can be no such thing as infinite growth on a finite planet.*[13]'

Eight of the 17 Sustainable Development Goals (SDGs)[14] of the United Nations refer to 'Natural Harmony': (3) Good Health and Well-being, (6) Clean Water and Sanitation, (7) Affordable and Clean Energy, (11) Sustainable Cities and Communities, (12) Responsible Consumption and Production, (13) Climate

Action, (14) Life Below Water, and (15) Life On Land. These eight well-defined, sustainable development goals can be adopted by citizens around the globe who wish to implement these goals. The United Nations can pay these citizen initiatives for their contributions, which would then also provide citizens with an income.

Citizens should be instructed to restore natural harmony by following three simple, measurable and achievable directives:

1. **End-to-end 100 percent recyclable.** All raw or used materials, products, services and processes that humankind chooses to use for any purpose, for any period and in any form must be 100 percent recyclable.

2. **Zero emissions and 100 percent biodegradable.** All raw or used materials, products, services and processes that humankind chooses to use for any purpose, for any period and in any form must have 0% emissions or pollution and be 100% biodegradable.

3. **Natural interest of 50 percent on loans from nature.** It should no longer be allowed to just take from nature for the sake of exploitation; it must be considered as a loan on which natural interest must be paid. Humankind must return all raw or used materials, products, services and processes to nature with 50 percent interest. For example, when taking two trees from nature, three trees must be paid back. This directive is mandatory until harmony with nature has been restored.

Many technological options are already available to help meet these directives, and investments in new technological advancements must be stimulated. For example, hydrogen is a 100 percent zero-emissions, renewable carrier of sustainable energy. However, it still has to compete with fossil fuel products and so the investment context for energy carriers must become favourable for clean hydrogen. Hydrogen has already been available for 75 years but it has not yet been embraced, as the (political, economic and fiscal) context still favours fossil fuels. As a result, current technologies do not yet allow massive production of hydrogen to meet our current and future energy needs.

As a point of departure, the seven fundamental system changes of the '*2020 Sustainability State of the Union*' (Jan Jonker, 2020)[15] can be formulated as follows:

1. Shift charging labour to the use of raw materials, and phase out fiscal benefits for the fossil fuel industry;
2. Include ecological and social values in economic decisions;
3. Work towards real prices that include all costs, such as CO2 emissions, nitrogen, pollution and a living wage;

4. Give more space to coexisting organisational forms of civilians and companies, for example in governing land and other 'commons';
5. Make producers responsible for the whole life cycle of products, including at the end of the cycle;
6. Tax wealth instead of labour, and reduce economic inequality;
7. Invest in liquidating companies that do not contribute to societal values by pricing and taxing, in combination with laws and regulations.

In order to restore natural living, fundamental societal measures need to be implemented by democratically elected UN members, including product pricing and taxation.

***Notes***

[1] Also called 'Placard of Abandonment'

[2] Originally the Dutch wanted to abandon the Spanish king and find a 'better ruler', but after two failed attempts they decided for pragmatic reasons to keep sovereignty in their own hands. It was only in 1648 that the declaration was officially acknowledged at the Treaty of Munster, when the Dutch Republic had already achieved European hegemony.

[3] In the Roman Empire, the category ***res communis*** referred to 'commons used and enjoyed by everyone', as opposed to ***res publica***, applied to government property (Basu, Jongerden, and Ruivenkamp (2017).

[4] Aristotle is credited as the first person to write about the 'wisdom of the crowd' in his work titled ***Politics***.

[5] Edward Posnett, The Sardex factor, Financial Times, September 18, 2015.

[6] Complementary Currency Resource Center, 'Online Database of Complementary Currency Systems Worldwide'. www.complementarycurrency.org.

[7] Interestingly, Wilkinson Richard G. and Kate Pickett's book 'The Spirit Level' has been published in 2009 and 2010 with three different subtitles: 'Why More Equal Societies Almost Always Do Better' (Allen Lane, 2009), 'Why Greater Equality Makes Societies Stronger', (US edition Bloomsbury Press, December 2009), and 'Why Equality is Better for Everyone' (Second edition, November 2010, Penguin Books).

[8] For an overview see Thomas B. Edsall, 'Just Right Inequality', ***The New York Times***, March 4, 2014.

[9] Kuznets, Simon, 'Does inequality in the distribution of income increase or decrease in the course of a country's economic growth?', Annual meeting of the American Economic Association, 1954.

[10] For example Casey Mulligan, 2012; Jonathan D. Ostry, Andrew Berg and Charalambos G. Tsangarides, 2014; Thomas Piketty, Emmanuel Saez and Stefanie Stantcheva, 2014; Robert J. Barro, 2008.

[11] See for example Casey Mulligan, 'The Redistribution Recession: How Labor Market Distortions Contracted the Economy', New York: Oxford University Press, 2012.

[12] Keen (2018) outlines five strategies: regulation, competitive innovation, consumer choice, civic responsibility and education. He argues that the combination of these five strategies with civil collaboration can help ensure an open, decentralised digital future to preserve our humanity in a digital world.

[13] Quote of Evert Bleijenberg, author of '***Swarm Organisation***: ***The vital next step in organisation development***' (2020).

[14] The 17 SDGs are: (1) No Poverty, (2) Zero Hunger, (3) Good Health and Well-being, (4) Quality Education, (5) Gender Equality, (6) Clean Water and Sanitation, (7) Affordable and Clean Energy, (8) Decent Work and Economic Growth, (9) Industry, Innovation and Infrastructure, (10) Reducing Inequality, (11) Sustainable Cities and Communities, (12) Responsible Consumption and Production, (13) Climate Action, (14) Life Below Water, (15) Life On Land, (16) Peace, Justice, and Strong Institutions, (17) Partnerships for the Goals.

[15] Jan Jonker, 'In the name of the economy we fight nature with a chain saw', ***The Netherlands Sustainability State of the Union***, September 1, 2020. 'The Netherlands Sustainability State of the Union' is an annual event that has been in existence since 2012.

# INVITATION TO ALL READERS FOR SUGGESTIONS

This book is meant to provide inspiration for building a vital and hopeful future for the next generations. It is the result of an intensive period of studying and understanding the current situation and imagining a better future society. To meet the first objective – understanding the current situation – I invested time in research and tested my observations and conclusions in lectures, presentations and meetings. The results are concisely formulated in the first six chapters, with the sixth chapter painting a picture of our future society – the *Elite Reset Society* – on the basis of current developments.

For the first six chapters I explored different trails of information, which involved digging into several scientific disciplines and societal domains, selecting the relevant information and then categorising the results. These were all academic activities I am used to performing and so it was an achievable task.

The second objective – imagining a better future society – was much more challenging. As is so often the case, understanding, analysing and formulating problems is something quite different from imagining a future that does not yet exist. The answer of most current critics on how to deal with societal problems and the future society that appears to be unfolding is to return to the past, to the society that has been. They typically do not provide a vision of a future society that will change as a result of multiple technological developments and their consequences.

In imagining a different and better society, I explored the emerging possibilities of new technologies, evaluating numerous new societal initiatives, reading future visions and collecting 'weak signals'. These sources of inspiration were inputs for the seventh chapter on the 'Glocal Citizens Society'. The main challenge was to step out of reality – especially amidst the 'Corona crisis' – and fundamentally redesign society. An exploration of this type never really ends and the text kept on changing and developing. However, there came a moment when it was time to stop and send the manuscript to the publisher. I did so in the knowledge that the current text is merely a snapshot of the unfolding future and that the book needs to become a living document.

With this book I give form to my strong desire to build a better society and I hope that the book inspires many readers to join me. I warmly welcome your feedback, ideas and support for improving this book. Suggestions for all chapters are welcome, with tips and recommendations aimed at strengthening the crucial seventh chapter especially appreciated. The best contributions will be included in future editions of the book. The names of the idea generators will be mentioned (with your approval) too, so if you would like be the co-creator of a better future, please join in.

I have opened the webpage **www.society4th.org** for collecting your valued input in the hope that this book is just the beginning. The beginning of a series of interactions. The beginning of a great book. And most of all: the beginning of creating a better future for the next generations.

# ACKNOW-LEDGEMENTS

I would like to thank everyone who has helped sharpen my mind.

Firstly, all of my colleagues at *Nyenrode Business University*, and particularly Bo van der Rhee, with whom I published a number of posts on corona mortality, Wolter Lemstra and Jeroen van der Velden. Secondly, my students, audiences at my presentations, friends and LinkedIn contacts. I am grateful for having been invited on board by the *Break-out Team* and the *Rainbow Team*. The members of these teams and I were able to pick up and carry our societal responsibility during the 'societal pandemic'. I appreciate the opportunity to work with all of these fantastic 'independent thinkers and doers'. Discussions with these teams have been very insightful.

A warm word of appreciation for my strategy consulting boutique *Strategy Works* colleagues Michael van Everdingen, Karel Koet, Christien van Rijs, Glen Schrijvers, Marco Kouters and Hans Lagaaij. They have always supported my journey to understand the future and kept *Strategy Works* services at the highest level for our clients while I isolated myself in my 'writing space'.

A special word of gratitude to my colleague and friend Evert Bleijenberg. A resident of my favourite writing location, Bonaire, former top manager and a professional deep water cinematographer, Evert contributed texts on swarms and on the state of our planet. We spent many hours discussing his book *Swarm Organisation* and the consequences for our future society.

Concept versions of the manuscript were reviewed by a team of 'counterreaders' (in alphabetical order): Christian Kromme, Evelien Ketelaar, Evert Bleijenberg, Ferenc van Damme, Hans Lagaaij, Jan Peter Balkenende, Jeroen den Uyl, Julia van Elten, Karel Koet, Madeleen Mulder, Marco Kouters, Michael van Everdingen, Steven de Waal and Trudy Huisman. Thank you all!

I am extremely grateful to my publisher, Sandra Britsemmer, for her courage in publishing this book, for her warm and professional attitude and for involving copy editor Danny Guinan and art director Gerard Hertsenberg. It has been a privilege to work with such a great and professional team at Vakmedianet!

I owe my greatest debt of gratitude to the love of my life, Pamela, with whom I have been happily married for 26 years now, and our daughter, Liz Bagheera. Without their love and support this manuscript would not have been possible.

# REFERENCES

Acemoglu, Daron, and James Robinson, *Comparative Politics*, Crown Business, 2012

Acemoglu, Daron, Simon Johnson and James Robinson, 'The Colonial Origins of Comparative Development: An Empirical Investigation', *American Economic Review*, 91 (5): 1369–1401, December 2001.

Acemoglu, Daron, and James Robinson, 'The Rise of Europe: Atlantic Trade, Institutional Change, and Economic Growth', *American Economic Review*, 95 (3): 546–579, June 2005.

Aristotle, *Politics*, Volume III, 1281b, Translated by H. Rackham, Loeb Classical Library 264.

Asimov, Isaac, 'Runaround', in: *I, Robot*, New York: Doubleday, 1950: p. 40.

Asimov, Isaac, *The Rest of the Robots*, New York: Doubleday, 1964.

Baase, Sara, *A Gift of Fire: Social, Legal, and Ethical Issues for Computing and the Internet*, 3rd edition, Prentice Hall, 2007.

Barro, Robert J., 2008. "*Inequality and Growth Revisited*', Asian Development Bank working paper, No. 11.

Barth, F. *Features of Person and Society under Agrarianism: Collected Essays. London*: Routledge & Kegan Paul, 2001.

Basu, Soutrik, Joost Jongerden, and Guido Ruivenkamp, Guido, 'Development of the drought tolerant variety Sahbhagi Dhan: exploring the concepts commons and community building', *International Journal of the Commons*, March 17, 2017, 11: 144.

Berle, Adolph A., and Gardiner C. Means, *The Modern Corporation, and Private Property*, Transaction Publishers, 1932

Bernish, C. The Illuminati Were Amateurs - The Facts Show These Five Families Rule the World, *The Free Thought Project*, 23 May 2016.

Betsill, Michele. M. & Elisabeth Corell. (2001), 'NGO Influence in International Environmental Negotiations: A Framework for Analysis', *Global Environmental Politics*, 2001 (4): 65-85.

Bigiotti, Alessandro & Alfredo Navarra, 'Optimizing Automated Trading Systems', *Advances in Intelligent Systems and Computing*, Springer International Publishing, October 19. 2018, pp. 254–261.

Bleijenberg, Evert, *Swarm Organisation: The vital next step in organisation development*, Bonaire: Swarm Organisation, 2020.

Bollier, David and Silke Helfrich (eds.), *Wealth of the Commons: A World Beyond Market and State*, Levellers Press, 2012.
Brannen, Peter, 'The Worst Times on Earth: Mass extinctions send us a warning', *Scientific American*, September 2020, pp. 74-88.
Brown, D.E. 1988. Hierarchy, History, and Human Nature: The Social Origins of Historical Consciousness. Tucson: University of Arizona Press.
Carneiro, R. L. (1981) 'The chiefdom: precursor of the state', in: G. D. Jones and R. R. Kautz (eds.) *The Transition to Statehood in the New World*, New York: Cambridge University Press, pp 37-79.
Carpenter, Charli, Sirin Duygulu, Alexander H. Montgomery & Anna Rapp, 'Explaining the Advocacy Agenda: Insights from the Human Security Network', *International Organization*, 2014, 68(2): 449-470;
Cohen, M. N. 1989, *Health and the Rise of Civilization*, New Haven: Yale University Press.
Coke, Edward Coke, '*Institutes of the Lawes of England*', 1628–1644.
Corporate Europe Observatory, '*ECJ confirms legality of unfair corporate tribunals in EU trade deals*', 30 April 2019.
Darwin, Charles (1859), *On the Origin of Species*, John Murray.
Davies, T. (2014). 'NGOs: *A New History of Transnational Civil Society*, New York: Oxford University Press.
DeLong, J. Bradford, 'Estimating World GDP, One Million B.C. – Present', working paper, Department of Economics, U.C. Berkeley, 26 February 2008.
Denning, Steve, Why Stakeholder Capitalism Will Fail, *Forbes*, January 5th, 2020.
De Waal, Steven, '*Civil Leadership as the Future of Leadership: Harnessing the disruptive power of citizens*', Wardy Poelstra Project management, 2018.
De Wit, B., *Strategy: An international perspective*, Cengage, 7th edition 2020.
Ford, Henry, and Samuel Crowther, *Today and Tomorrow*, Garden City Publishing Company, 1926.
Foreign Affairs Trade and Development, Government of Canada, 'Eli Lilly and Company versus Government of Canada', January 20, 2017.
Freeman, Richard; Griggs, Steven; Boaz, Annette, 'The practice of policy making', *Evidence & Policy*, Vol. 7, Iss. 2, May 2011: 127-136.
Frey, Carl B., and Michael Osborne, The Future of Employment: How susceptible are jobs to computerisation?, *Technological Forecasting and Social Change*, 114: 254-280, 17 September 2013.
Friedman, Milton, 'The Social Responsibility of Business is to Increase its Profits', *The New York Times Magazine*, September 13, 1970.
Galton, F. 'Vox populi', *Nature*, 75 (1949): 450–451.
Gould, Stephen J., (2002), The Structure of Evolutionary Theory, Belknap Harvard, Harvard.
Hamilton, Isobel Asher, 'Elon Musk believes AI could turn humans into an endangered species like the mountain gorilla', *Business Insider*, 26 November 2018.

Harari, Yuval Noah, *Homo Sapiens: A Brief History of Humankind*, Vintage Publishing, 2006.

Harari, Yuval Noah, *Homo Deus: A Brief History of Tomorrow*, Vintage Publishing, 2017

Harari, Yuval Noah, 'The world after coronavirus', *Financial Times*, March 20, 2020.

Hardin, Garrett (1968), 'The Tragedy of the Commons', *Science*, 162 (3859): 1243–1248.

High Representative of the Union for Foreign Affairs of the European Commission *'Tackling COVID-19 disinformation - Getting the facts'*, Brussels, 10 June 2020.

Johnson, A. W., *'The Evolution of Human Societies: from Foraging Group to Agrarian State'*, Stanford: Stanford University Press, 2000.

Jonker, Jan, 'In the name of the economy, we fight nature with a chainsaw. Seven tools for a different approach', *The Netherlands Sustainability State of the Union*, September 1, 2020. (Original text in Dutch: 'We gaan uit naam van de economie de natuur met een kettingzaag te lijf. Zeven breekijzers om het anders te doen').

Kaku, Michio, *'The Future of the Mind: The Scientific Quest to Understand, Enhance, and Empower the Mind'*, Anchor Books, 2015.

Kant, Immanuel, *'Perpetual Peace: A Philosophical Sketch'*, 1795.

Karns, M.P. 'Nongovernmental organization', In: *Encyclopaedia Britannica*, 24 February 2020.

Keck, Margaret E. & Kathryn Sikkink, 'Transnational Advocacy Networks in International and Regional Politics', *International Social Science Journal*, 1999, 51 (159), 89-101.

Keen, Andrew, *'How to Fix the Future: Staying Human in the Digital Age'*, Atlantic Books, 2018.

Khan, Lina M. 'The Separation of Platforms and Commerce', *Columbia Law Review*, 119 (4): 973, 2019.

Khan, Lina M, 'Amazon's Antitrust Paradox', *The Yale Law Journal*, Volume 126, Nr. 3, January 2017, pp. 564-907.

Kuznets, Simon, *'Does inequality in the distribution of income increase or decrease in the course of a country's economic growth?'*, Annual meeting of the American Economic Association, 1954.

Landemore, Hélène, 'Collective Wisdom – Old and New', in: Landemore, Hélène; Elster, Jon (eds.), *Collective wisdom: principles and mechanisms*, Cambridge: Cambridge University Press, 2012.

Langlois, S. 2001. "Traditions: Social." In Neil J. Smelser and Paul B. Baltes, Editors, International Encyclopedia of the Social & Behavioral Sciences, Pergamon, Oxford, 15829-15833.

Lemke, Thomas. P. and Gerald T. Lins (eds.), *Soft Dollars and Other Trading Activities*, Thomson West, 2015–2016.

Lenski, Gerhard. "Agrarian Societies [Parts I & II]." In Power and Privilege: A Theory of Social Stratification, 189-296. 1966. Reprinted, Chapel Hill: University of North Carolina Press, 1984.

Lewis, David, 'Nongovernmental Organizations, Definition and History', *Political Science*, 2009.

Licklider, 'Man-Computer Symbiosis', *Transactions on Human Factors in Electronics*, volume HFE-1, pp. 4–11, March 1960

Lopatto, E. 'Elon Musk unveils Neuralink's plans for brain-reading 'threads' and a robot to insert them', *The Verge*, 16 July 2019.

Lorenz, Edward N. 'Deterministic Nonperiodic Flow', *Journal of the Atmospheric Sciences*, March 1963, 20 (2): 130–141.

Lorenz, Jan, Heiko Rauhut, Frank Schweitzer, and Dirk Helbing, 'How social influence can undermine the wisdom of crowd effect', *Proceedings of the National Academy of Sciences of the United States of Amerika (PNAS)*, 31 May 2011, 108 (22) 9020-9025.

Machiavelli, Niccolò, *The Art of War* (L'arte della guerra), 1521

MacInnes, T., Tinson, A. Hughes, C. Born, T.B. and Aldridge, H., 'Monitoring poverty and social exclusion', *New Policy Institute*, London, November 23, 2015.

Markoff, J. 'Elon Musk's Company Takes Baby Steps to Wiring Brains to the Internet', *The New York Times*. July 16, 2019.

Michels, Robert, 'Political Parties: A Sociological Study of the Oligarchical Tendencies of Modern Democracy', 1915, trans. Eden and Cedar Paul (Kitchener, Ontario: Batoche Books, 2001).

Motta, Erick V.S. Kasie Raymann, and Nancy A. Moran, 'Glyphosate perturbs the gut microbiota of honey bees', *Proceedings of the National Academy of Sciences*, September 24, 2018.

Mulligan, Casey, '*The Redistribution Recession: How Labor Market Distortions Contracted the Economy*', New York: Oxford University Press, 2012.

Newitz, A., 'Elon Musk is setting up a company that will link brains and computers', *Ars Technica*. March 27, 2017.

Nolan, Patrick, and Gerhard Lenski. 2014. "The Agricultural Economy." In Human Societies: An Introduction to Macrosociology, 156-201. 12th ed. New York: Oxford University Press.

North, Douglass and Barry Weingast, 'Constitutions and Commitment: The Evolution of Institutions Governing Public Choice in Seventeenth-Century England', *Journal of Economic History*, 49 (4): 803–832, December 1989.

North, Douglass, John Wallis, and Barry Weingast, 'Violence and the Rise of Open-Access Orders', *Journal of Democracy*, 20 (1): 55–68, January 2009.

OECD, 'Income inequality', *OECD Insights*, 2015.

Ostrom, Elinor, *Governing the Commons: The Evolution of Institutions for Collective Action*, Cambridge University Press, 1990.

Ostry, Jonathan D., Andrew Berg and Charalambos G. Tsangarides, 'Redistribution, Inequality, and Growth', *International Monetary Fund*, February 2014.

Pabortsava, Katsiaryna & Richard S. Lampitt, 'High concentrations of plastic hidden beneath the surface of the Atlantic Ocean', *Nature Communications*, Volume 11, 18 August 2020.

Page, Scott E. (2007), '*The Difference: How the Power of Diversity Creates Better Groups, Firms, Schools, and Societies*', Princeton, NJ: Princeton University Press
Piketty, Thomas, Emmanuel Saez and Stefanie Stantcheva, 'Optimal Taxation of Top Labor Incomes', *American Economic Journal: Economic Policy*, Vol. 6, No. 1, February 2014, pp. 230-271.
Piketty, T. '*Capital in the Twenty-First Century*', Boston: Harvard Business School Press, 2014.
Posnett, Edward, 'The Sardex factor', *Financial Times*, September 18, 2015.
Prpić, John; Shukla, Prashant P.; Kietzmann, Jan H.; McCarthy, Ian P., 'How to work a crowd: Developing crowd capital through crowdsourcing', *Business Horizons*, 2015, 58 (1)
Pryor, F. L. 2006. "The Adoption of Agriculture: Some Theoretical and Empirical Evidence." American Anthropologist 88:879-97.
Renfrew, C. (ed.) 1993. The Explanation of Culture Change. Pittsburgh: University of Pittsburgh Press.
Rifkin, J. (2011), *The Third Industrial Revolution: How Lateral Power is Transforming Energy, the Economy, and the World*, London: Pelgrave Mc Millan.
Risse, Thomas, 'Transnational Actors and World Politics', In: Carlsnaes, Walter, Thomas Risse & Beth Simmons (eds.), *Handbook of International Relations*, 2013, London: Sage Publications, 426-452.
Service, Elman Rogers (1962), Primitive social organization: an evolutionary perspective, Random House.
Schwab, K. (2015). "The Fourth Industrial Revolution, What It Means and How to Respond", *Foreign Affairs*, 12 December.
Schwab, K. (2016), *The Fourth Industrial Revolution*, New York: Crown Publishing Group.
Schwaab, *The Global Reset: The Case for Stakeholder Capitalism*, John Wiley & Sons Inc, 30 December 2020.
Schwab, K. and T. Malleret, *COVID-19: The Great Reset*, Agentur Schweiz, 9 July 2020.
Sheikh, Haroon, '*Hydropolitics: cooperation and conflict on seven seas*' (in Dutch), Boom, 2019.
Smith, Madeleine, David C. Love, Chelsea M. Rochman, and Roni A. Neff, 'Microplastics in Seafood and the Implications for Human Health', *Current Environmental Health Report*, August 16, 2018; 5(3): 375–386.
Statt, Nick, 'Kernel is trying to hack the human brain – but neuroscience has a long way to go', *The Verge*, Feb 22, 2017.
Steinfeld, Henning, Pierre Gerber, Tom Wassenaar, Vincent Castel, Mauricio Rosales, and Cees de Haan, 'Livestock's Long Shadow: Environmental issues and options', *Food and Agriculture Organization of the United Nations*, 2006.
Streitfeld, David, 'Amazon's Antitrust Antagonist Has a Breakthrough Idea', *The New York Times*, September 7, 2018.
Subramanian, Arvind, '*Which Nations Failed*', The American Interest, October 30, 2012.

Sun Tzu, '*The Art of War*' (5th Century BC).
Surowiecki, James, *The Wisdom of Crowds*, Doubleday, 2004.
Susskind, R. and Daniel Susskind, 2017, *The Future of the Professions: How Technology Will Transform the Work of Human Experts*, Oxford University Press.
The Canadian Press, 'Ottawa sued over Quebec fracking ban: company's suit based on NAFTA provisions', *CBC News*, Nov 23, 2012.
Thompson, Paul B. *The Agrarian Vision: Sustainability and Environmental Ethics*, Lexington: University of Kentucky Press, 2010.
United Nations Conference on Trade And Development (UNCTAD), '*Recent Developments in Investor-State Dispute Settlement (ISDS): Updated for the Multilateral Dialogue on Investment*', 28-29 May 2013.
Van Lotringen, Cees, *Up to here and no further: The Netherlands on the threshold of a new era* (Original text in Dutch: Tot hier en niet verder: Nederland op de drempel van een nieuwe tijd), Writers United, 2018.
Von Clausewitz, Karl, '*On War*' (1832).
Von Krockow, Graf Christian, 'Difficult Neighbourship. On the history and future of Dutch-German Relationships' ('Schwierige Nähe. Zur Geschichte und Zukunft der Deutsch-Niederländischen Beziehungen'; 'Moeilijk nabuurschap: over de geschiedenis en toekomst van de Duits-Nederlandse betrekkingen'), Huizinga Lezing, 1993.
Voitchovski, S. (2009), 'Inequality and Economic Growth', In: Salverda, W., Nolan, B., and Smeeding, T.M., *The Oxford Handbook of Economic Inequality*, Oxford University Press, Oxford.
Weatherford, Jack, 'Genghis Khan and the Quest for God: How the World's Greatest Conqueror Gave Us Religious Freedom', Penguin, 2016.
Wilkinson Richard G. and Kate Pickett, '*The Spirit Level: Why More Equal Societies Almost Always Do Better*', Allen Lane, 2009.
Wilkinson Richard G. and Kate Pickett, '*The Spirit Level: Why Greater Equality Makes Societies Stronger*', US edition, Bloomsbury Press, December 2009.
Wilkinson Richard G. and Kate Pickett, '*The Spirit Level: Why Equality is Better for Everyone*', Second edition, November 2010, Penguin Books.
World Inequality Lab (2018), *World Inequality Report 2018*, Paris.
Yi, Sheng Kung Michael; Steyvers, Mark; Lee, Michael D.; Dry, Matthew J., 'The Wisdom of the Crowd in Combinatorial Problems', *Cognitive Science*, April 2012, 36 (3): 452–47.

# RESUMÉ
# BOB DE WIT

Prof. Bob de Wit is a visionary academic and Professor of Strategic Leadership at the Nyenrode Center for Strategy, Organization & Leadership. His main research topic is the transformation of companies, industries and societies in relation to digital technologies, biotechnology and sustainable energy solutions. Bob is a globally recognised inspirational speaker, delivering presentations and keynote addresses to large audiences. His aim is to prepare private and public leaders for the economic and societal revolution in the years ahead.

Bob has (co-)authored many books, articles, chapters, cases and teaching notes in the area of strategic management. Editions of his book *Strategy: An International Perspective* (1994, 1998, 2005, 2010, 2014, 2017, 2020) can be found at universities and business schools in over 70 countries across the globe. Bob's books are categorised as the 'paradox school of thought in strategy'.

Bob has taught in over 50 countries across all continents. His teaching focuses on C-level executives and non-executive board members in courses such as Non-Executive Programme, New Board Programme, Executive MBA, General Management Programme and Strategic Leadership Programme and in a variety of dedicated executive teaching programmes. He has received numerous teaching awards from Nyenrode Business University, Maastricht University and the Rotterdam School of Management.

Bob de Wit holds a bachelor's degree in Psychology from Utrecht University, a master's degree from IIB Delft and a PhD in Management Science from Erasmus University Rotterdam. From 1986 to 1996, he was a professor of strategic management at the Rotterdam School of Management, and from 1996 to 2012 Professor of Strategy and Associate Dean for Research at the Maastricht School of Management. He has been a member of the Advisory Board of the Journal of Change Management and of the Strategic Management Society Review Board.

Bob de Wit is the founding director (1998) of *Strategy Works*, a strategy consulting firm and *Strategy Academy*, which designs and delivers in-company (digital) leadership programmes.

Printed in Great Britain
by Amazon

86509505R00060